MINE

Diamond Frances

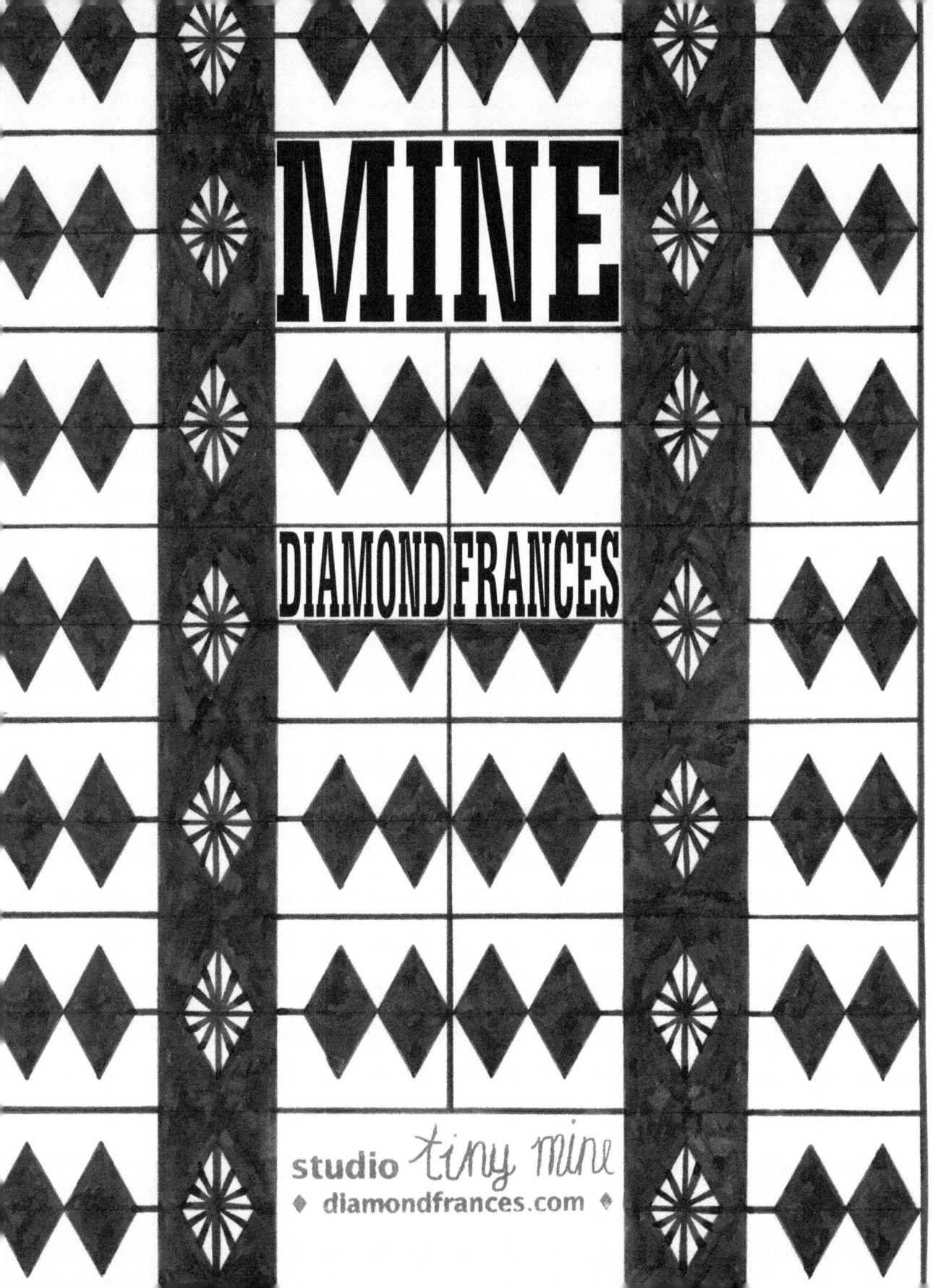

MINE

DIAMOND FRANCES

studio *tiny mine*
◆ diamondfrances.com ◆

for The Mathematician

SUPPORT CREATIVE ARTS

ISBN-13: 978-1542971867
ISBN-10: 1542971861

a TINY MINE production

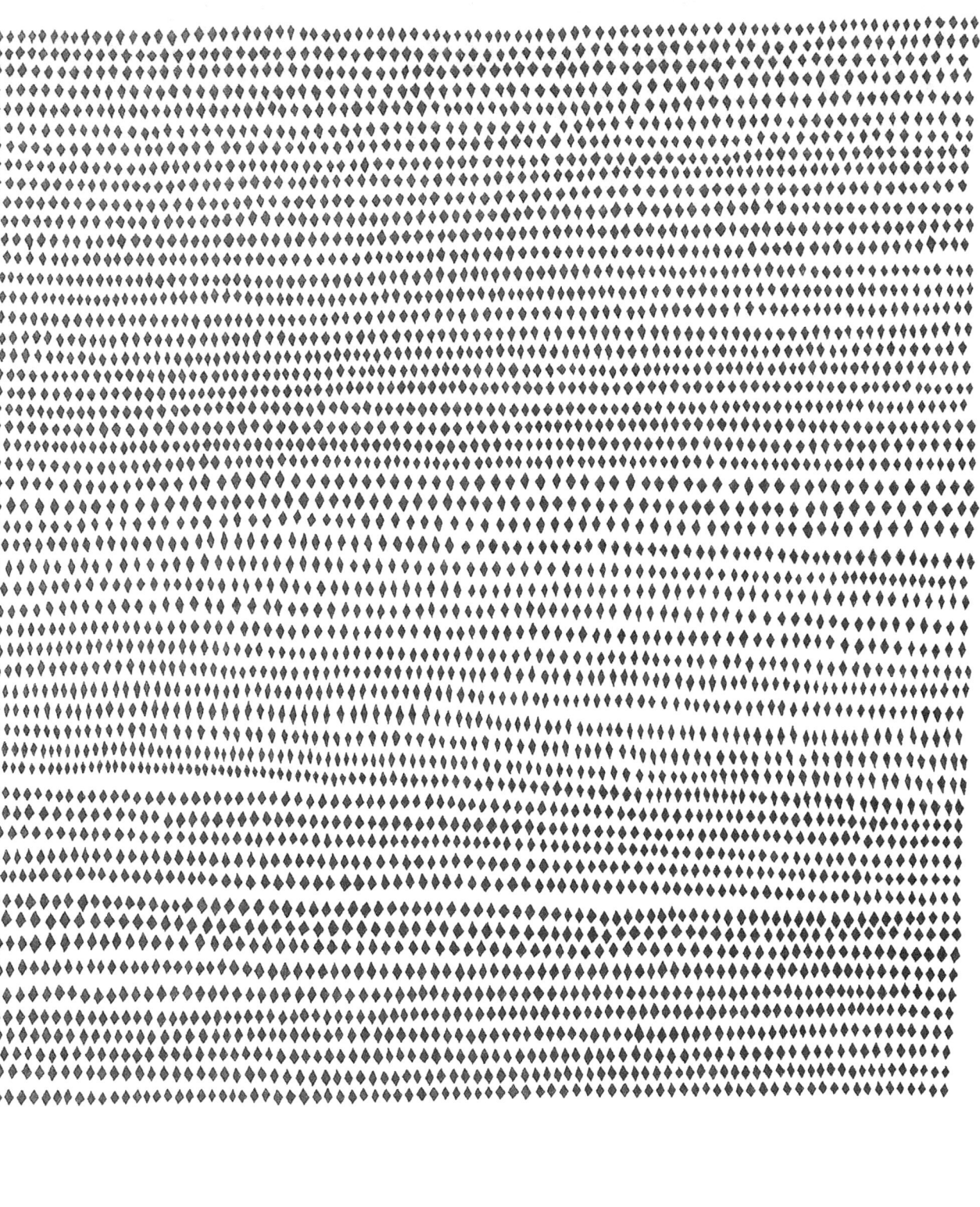

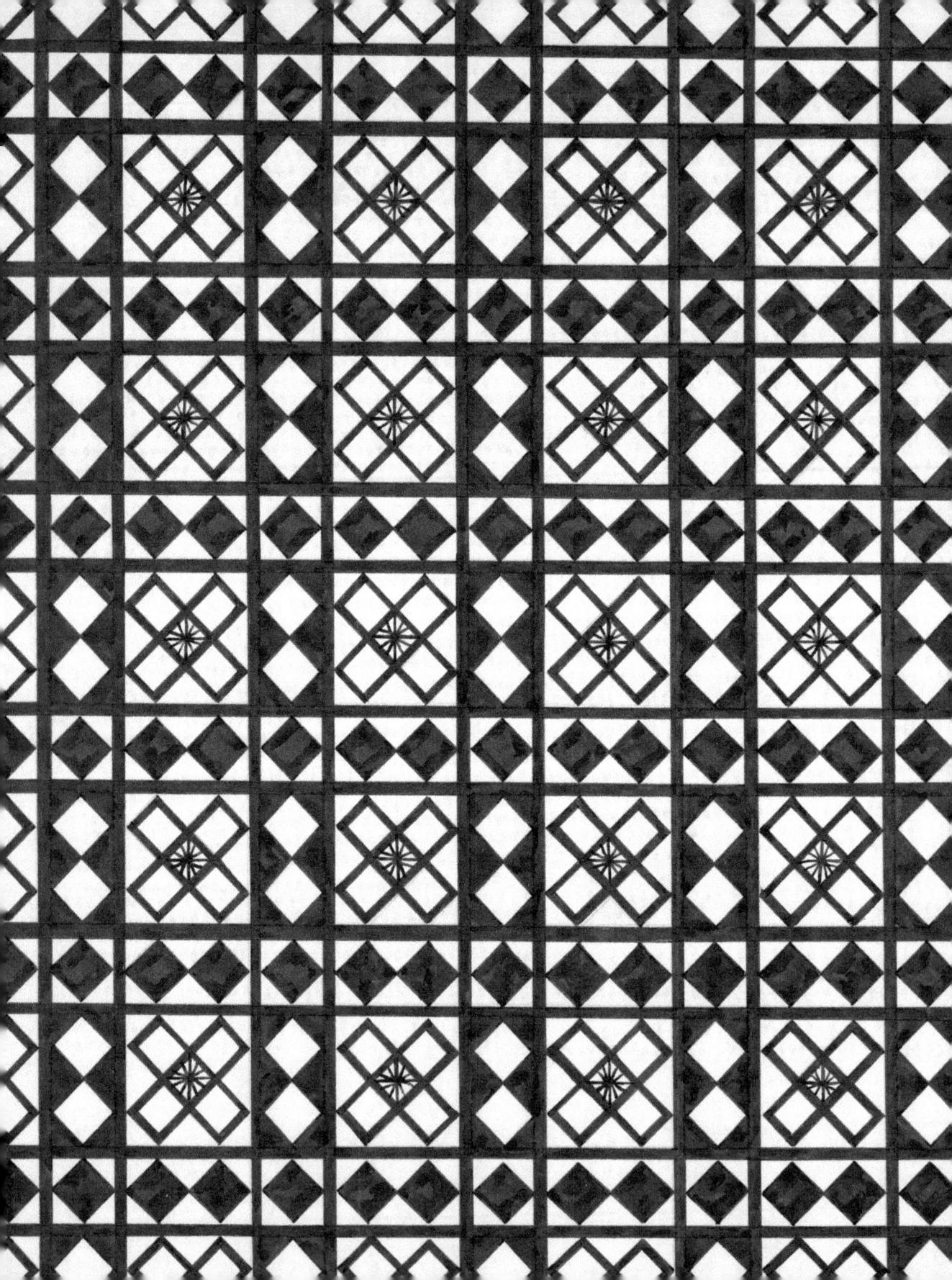

BLUE GROUND

I was born in the Austrian mountains forty years ago, second of five girls and my father was on the ships most of the time. My mother, four sisters and two grandmothers and one great-grandmother formed an all women enclave.

The village of my birth is small and I went to primary school and secondary school there. In winter I would go skiing every day after school and on weekends with my younger sister Regina and Margit, our neighbour. I remember getting my first ever skis for Christmas. They were hidden in the corner and I was crying because I thought I didn't get anything from the "Christkindl" (Santa Claus) that year. But they were perfect, red shiny Kneissl skis with a white outlined star. The other present I remember clearly was a fake leather, royal blue doll's pram. It was the old fashioned style which at the time, in the eighties, was probably the only style. I got it for my birthday and there was a bed sheet on it as wrapping because it was so big. It stood in our living room. I loved that one too. And a white bike. Great white bike.

I must have left the pram at my neighbours house once I

got bored playing with it and never wondered about it ever again. It just vanished into a vacuum called indifference. Toys do get old. My mother didn't notice either, she was working at the hotel most of the time and she didn't keep track of our lives. Granny Ria looked after us. Nothing ever mattered much.

That's not really true. There were lots of good things in my childhood. We were bored sometimes but my sister Regina told me years later that playing with me was always the most fun. I was surprised to hear that because my older and younger sisters often ganged up on me. Once they pushed me over and I fell into my watercolour paints on the floor. Then I would run downstairs to the cellar, where my room was; next to the sauna and grandma's bedroom. It was alright but a bit dark. Not much daylight. My oldest sister's room was the original kids room on the ground floor, where we all slept when we were smaller and Regina's was on the first floor. She got one of the guest rooms. There were rooms on the top floor too but they were rented out for holiday guests. It's the Austrian mountains after all. Many normal houses have guest rooms. I ran in

2

my room and locked the door and cried. I had a little pink sports bag and I used to pretend to pack my bag and leave. I did that regularly. I also liked playing with Barbie. I didn't loose my skis. I lost earrings. My other grandmother, Granny Mary, my mum's mum, gave me earrings with one ruby, one sapphire and one emerald. No diamond. I wished I would still have them. They were beautiful. I lost them to eternity. I think Margit has them. That's were I lost them. A bench outside their house, they fell on the floor, I cannot remember the details maybe there was a gap that went down another level. I couldn't find them and went home. I wished I would have had another go at finding them the next day or something.

Regina and I were at Margit's house pretty much every day or she was over at our place. My grandmother often told her to go home and ask why she is always here and if she doesn't have a home. Granny Ria was like that. Regina and I told her to stop saying those things and our friend just ignored her.

Margit's father was a carpenter and her mom was a

waitress. She smoked a lot and Margit got into smoking from an early age. We, my sister and I tried it too. Hiding in the forest or behind the house but we never were that into it. I wonder if she is still smoking today. I started smoking later when I was older but I think Margit just kept going from being about ten or twelve.

I get mixed up with my memories. I do have the memories but I don't have a good grasp on time. What happened when gets muddled up sometimes.

Walking with my sisters and mother. My mother liked going for thirty to forty minute walks regularly, every day. I assume she still does. When we were in Kindergarten my mum drove us by car. Sometimes my father would drive us. That must have been when he was home from the ships. We screamed and cried and hung onto my mums skirt. I didn't want him to take me. He must have felt bad about that. Children are cruel. I had a beautiful white winter coat when I was in Kindergarten. It was off white woolly and came to just under my knees. It had a hood with a beige fake fur trim and two big pompoms hanging off a string by the neck.

I felt like an Eskimo princess. It was beautiful. In Kindergarten, I was very quiet and shy when I spoke to the teachers and I was really loudly shouting at the other children when they annoyed me. The teachers told me off about that. They didn't like me.

When I was a bit older, a teenager in Kössen, the village, I had another friend, Bettina. She lived in a different part of the village and I had to ride my bike to see her. She was the total opposite of me but we did spent some time together for some reason. Her parents got drunk sometimes. They played tennis in their spare time. The teachers from my school played tennis too. All this was totally different to my world. My parents were more normal than that. Bettina was training to be a hairdresser. She had a boyfriend who got drunk and he looked a bit rough. He was from St. Johann the closest town. Bettina had big breasts and very blond curly hair. I was the opposite of that. When Bettina was in primary school in my class, she wore a dark blue seventies suit. It looked very strict and this was the eighties. I fixed up her outfit, she let me. I rolled up the trousers and sleeves of her suit. I was into clothes. My mother took us twice a year to a town in Germany. Forty minutes by car and we all, three sisters got lots of new clothes from a department store. We used to get most things we wanted. No brands. I never wore branded clothes, didn't really know anything about them. On the way home we always went to Mc Donald's Drive In. We loved it. One day my mother took the other way out of town, not past the Drive In. We bothered her and didn't stop moaning and nagging and she had to turn round so we could have our burgers. When my father came too he would say no. There was not going to be McDonald's and there was no arguing. We, the girls didn't like that. He always said no.

We also had mail order catalogues in the house. My sister and I had a pastime of flicking through the entire catalogue and choosing things we wanted on each page. The person who points to the favourite item first wins it. Great fun. Lots of pages didn't have anything we wanted but we did the entire catalogue anyway.

Another thing I remember doing was crocheting an entire ball of wool. just one big string of crocheting line and then wrapping it around the furniture as many times as I could. There were three big chairs and a couch but I didn't do the couch. I think it went around about three times. What a fantastic pastime.

I did not drink alcohol at all. When I went to the disco in Kufstein, I danced the entire time and have one water. My sisters had boyfriends so I had no one to go out with. I went all by myself in the car. Must have been eighteen. Eighteen years old.

I went to tourism school and every summer we had to get work experience. One summer, I think I was sixteen or seventeen, I worked as nanny in France. They let me try wine, drink wine with my dinners and I really loved it. I loved wine. I loved the French. I brought home speciality cheese. The mum helped me buy them, my favourite ones. Back at home the specialness was lost. It was a total downer, the cheese. Nobody wanted to even try it. It got forgotten at the back of the fridge. Old hard weird goats cheese. I continued to eat like the family ate in France because I liked it but I stopped doing that soon. It just didn't make any sense. Totally out of context. Back to my normal life.

I bought my first packet the summer I worked in Hamburg in Germany and smoked it excitedly by myself in the park. I thought it was pretty cool. My friend Sylvia smoked sometimes. That's why I started. She was cooler than me. And, she was also in Hamburg that summer and it bothered her that I was there too. She stayed with her uncle and worked at the Marriott hotel. Her uncle was sort of the boss there I think. We saw each other three times over the entire stay there which is weird considering we were best friends and shared a flat at school time in St. Johann. I thought of her as my best friend but she had her best friends in her home town.

There was also Silke. She was always nice to me. After school finished, when I was 19, we came to London together. We found a job as waitresses. Silke did go back to Austria after a few months because she was going to be a stewardess and I stayed.

One day, walking in the rain along Charing Cross Road I saw a big long coat all the way to the floor from the corner of my eye. I was under my umbrella. I turned round to look again. Then I looked up at the building the boy just came out from. It said Central Saint Martins School. Weirdly, I went in. very unlike me and totally out of character. I picked up a brochure from the reception and I would read this booklet about a hundred times from cover to cover. It was so exciting. I did have enough money saved up to pay for an introduction course that went on for a few weeks. I was very good. We made mood boards and designed our own collections. I loved it. On my last assignment I got 120%. The other two girls who were good went for interviews with Louise Wilson and got into the course. I wished now I would have at least gone for the interview just to meet the formidable Louise Wilson. At the time I didn't know anything about her, just that she was scary. Only later did I read articles about how great she was and now she is dead. I never thought I could go to school, afford it. I already had a job as assistant for a pattern cutter. Mainly I was a runner. We made costumes for theatre and movies. I was often holding the pins while seeing famous actors and running around Carnaby Street bringing clothes to all the Malaysian and Cypriot tailors and get button holes made in a little downstairs shop in Soho.

Weirdly, the same thing happened again later. I still had my job and never did much apart from of that. No friends, never any friends really. No going out, just sitting in my flat basically. Wasted youth I would call it.

My littlest sister came to visit over the summer. She took my job for the time I was doing another foundation course. This time at the Slade School of Fine Art as I had already done a few shorter courses there. I loved it again and this time I went for the interview knowing that I wouldn't be able to study. I even told all the other students about it and the girl who was on number 6, I think they took 5 of us was really counting on me declining.

I was lucky my boss said to me at the time: The Slade is famous. If they take you you have to go. And I did. I did! I was so happy. I got to keep my job part time so I still earned enough money to get by. I was naive, stupid. I thought it was all about the art so I never hung out with my fellow students. Did not occur to me I have no idea why. I did like them. I never went to a single party. I was so stupid. I am still stupid or poorly equipped but it doesn't matter anymore. I needed somebody to tell me to go but I didn't have that. I wouldn't really have been able to afford it. Going out in London costs a lot. I never practised having friends so I couldn't do it.

It's like being paralysed. I am in a bad situation and I know it's not good for me but I cannot do anything. I must have somebody to say it, to tell me what to do. Only then am I free to act. I have no idea what this is. It's not good.

My Austrian family crushed me. They crushed every diamond inside of me since I was a little girl. They are nice and they don't mean any harm. They are not nice, actually. They are not evil and they don't mean any harm. They don't mean to be evil but they are and they do mean to do harm but they don't know it. They crushed the spirit. The energy gets sucked out of the body like the juice from a Capri Sun drink. Drained. When I come out I am lifeless. For weeks, months. I slowly need to rebuild what I think is me. All values, everything that's exciting and worthwhile in my life, has been taken out of me. It's not important and nothing matters, also not for themselves or anybody else. I am not the only one but I am the only one who cares. I am so desperate for meaning and value. I want something to be important and I want the obsession. That's all the essence otherwise I am only furniture. I don't want that. What about love and care. And hot water and a cosy toasty living room. Full cupboards and birthday parties and effort to do things that don't have to be done but make it better. Not just the bare essentials and nothing more. Sitting, drinking coffee. The cold huge house and the hotel kitchen with a weird high table made from some type of industrial grey metal looking material. Food everywhere but not in a good way. Huge pots, old food in all the industrial fridge drawers. Old gas ovens and a deep fryer. Huge industrial mixing machine and other frying stuff. I used to make Christmas cookies there. Huge patches so you get tired of doing it. Not with butter but margarine. Great-grandma Rosina used real butter always. She had a hang up about real butter because of the war when there was none or not enough. She told us how they told their mom when she went down into the cellar. "Thin bread, THICK butter!" She always gave us thick butter on our bread. She used to cut it in slices and lay it on the bread. Especially the Christmas fruit bread, Klotzenbrot. I loved that. And she brushed everybody's long hair for a very long time with a very soft brush. Me and my two sisters. That was quite nice, a bit boring maybe.

Lots of good memories but they crushed me. Or maybe I crushed them. Maybe I am asking for too much. The warm room and the too hot water. And all the extra. I am mean. I am sorry to be so mean.

I wish my father was around sometimes. He is always grumpy and distant. One day he will die and if there is time before that I am not even gonna go and see him then. I will be sad and feel like I have let him down. Really, he is nice, he just cannot show it, that's my secret fantasy belief. He is not like my mother and sisters. They don't care if they never see me again. I don't know what my mother thinks but nobody will ever know that. She is my mother and that is supposed to be important but that's the myth we get told on TV and everywhere else. Family matters and it's the most important thing in the world. But this can't be true for everybody. Many families are outright destructive. They actually physically harm members. Some families kill their members so it's not true that you always have to go back. I wished it was different and I still feel bad because nothing about this entire situation is that clear for me. Maybe I just imagined all these feelings and I am really mean and unfair. Nobody makes any effort to see me though, they do have my email address. They must be fine. I wasn't there since I was nineteen really. And later, in my thirties I told them I will never come back. My mother sent me a note saying she will let me go. It was a very strange note which was in an envelope with some other unimportant mail she forwarded to me. It could never be just the letter with her. That would be showing too much effort. It always has to look like we don't really matter much.

I like to take a diamond nap. I love sleeping. I am not good with people. I am rude without meaning to be. I am shy and scared and quiet. I leave a room without saying anything. I am scared to talk but also probably don't care enough.

Don't care about much. They think I am rude. I am rude. I probably offend everyone I meet. Fortunately I do not meet a lot of people. I avoid people. That makes me rude too and indifferent. Everybody else becomes friendly to each other eventually. I always stay on the outside. Looking in. Watching. People run from me, literally. They want nothing to do with me.

It's bad, very bad. Really. I will go and have a lay down now. It is all too much.

diamond cracking day. get up at crack of dawn. make tea. sit down. write in diary. observe. get started. get interrupted by daughter. breakfast. walk walk the boy to school. the hardest bit of my day is it to get the smallest ready for school. he needs to be touched with diamond gloves only. walk walk. pushing the pram. come back. work. cook and eat lunch with husband. nap. have a tea. walk walk. children. bouncing daughter on a ball, making snack, sitting on couch with them, and the oldest one too. chat a bit. do some work on and off. do other things like internet shopping. try and get the little one to have his bath, make dinner, clean the dishes, bring littlest to bed. get the girl and bring her to bed. work a bit more or waste time. my oldest takes himself to bed. sit at my desk until husband comes to watch TV on couch. shower. go to bed.

As far as I remember there was snow every winter. Sometimes we had to wait for it and were hoping it would snow for Christmas. That's the year I am thinking of, the year it snowed on Christmas eve. My sister, Margit and I went skiing every day after school and on weekends. We lived close to the lifts, a five minute walk away. The following event happened earlier, when we were younger. I remember wearing my snow outfit, a ski-overall with lots of layers underneath to keep me warm. We were sliding off a little hill at the bottom of the mountain. You cannot go home. Once you go home you are not going back. Us three girls, we had been there for a while already but now we started to feel the urge to take a pee. We were discussing what to do. It seemed to be a real problem and we decided. We would sit down on the snow and just pee. It was awful. I still remember how bad that felt. The cold snow and the warm pee and the soaking pants. I cannot picture the yellow patch in the snow but there must have been one. And now we had to go home anyway. At least we didn't need to pee urgently on the way home. I have no idea what Ria Oma (grandma) must have thought when she saw our clothes. Probably that we peed in our pants.

Margit had a garage roof top not too high. We used to jump off that into a big pile of snow and then our boots got stuck and I had real trouble getting them out.

I played Barbie quite a bit. Sometimes we took our Barbies with some equipment and accessories to the Unterberg, the mountain. The path we took went up the other side. Not where the ski slopes were but on the side where the trees were. It was summer anyway. There was a little water running downhill, a little stream, quite small really. We set up Barbie's living area and I took her for a swim and put her in the water. Barbie got away from me. She was going downhill fast and I really had to run after her. I thought that was it for my Barbie, that she was headed off somewhere far away from me. I was scared to loose her and ran down the steep mountain after her. That was dangerous for me too. Then she got stuck. I didn't let her go swimming again.

There was a fake ice rink in Kössen. Not a real lake. There is a big lake in the next village Walchsee. We didn't have our own skating shoes but you could rent them. That was a bit of a longer walk and it was really very cold. Thirty or forty minutes walk. There was a tiny hut were you would get your skates and it would be lovely and warm and you could get a hot chocolate, but it was freezing outside. We had been there too long and now we had to walk home. Our fingers and hands were frozen and our face and hair had frozen breath on it. If hair goes frozen it's awful. I was so cold. That was the coldest I have ever been.

In winter Ria Oma always made fire in the house. It was a tiled stove. There was no switch for instant heat. There was normal central heating too but this was different. Heat from real fire. The stove door is in the hallway, it takes skill to get the fire going. And it needs to be done about three hours before you want it nice and warm in the living room, maybe even six hours. She had her spot there on the bench attached to it. Sitting. She also took her naps there. Nice warm tiles. It's the most beautiful cosiness there is in the entire world. And the room stays heated for six to eight hours after. We used to climb on it and dry our ski clothes at the top. My father put his apples on there so they go nice and leathery. Really. They are good apples. Boskop apples. Real fire and real wood. It takes effort. When she was dead, there was very little of that heat. I left her, I moved out to the little flat at the back of the hotel with my older sister. Grandma could be mean, she never was mean to me, and annoying and she gave me no privacy and let the cat onto my bed. I didn't like the cat on my bed. She once asked me, later, when I came to see her: Is it true you moved out because of me? My mother must have said that to her. She must have been hurt. A lot. I am sorry.

I got a big box of coloured pencils when I was little. From my mother. They came in a metal box, the brand was Jolly. It was so amazing, I loved it. It looks much better if the pencils stack in the right order. When the colours don't match it looks a bit of a mess. I also loved that shop next to school. Stationery. All colours of ink cartridges for my fountain pen. And a light pink puffy pencil case with diamond stitching. It had a zip and then there were rubber bands stitched down to hold pens, rulers, rubbers and sharpeners, areas for coloured pencils and graphite pencils. This is were I spent my spare time before school started because the bus arrived at school before it was open. It was the only option apart from standing outside the school waiting. The other thing I did after getting off the bus was walking to the bakery and pretty much every day I got myself a raisin bread.

My mother took me to the village shoe shop. New shoes for school! There were green turquoise ones with a buckle at the front and royal blue ballerina with a half bow at the side. My mother really thought the green ones were much better and she tried very hard to get me to take those. I insisted on liking the blue ones a lot more and I spent an awful lot of time trying to convince her to buy the blue shoes for me. And I succeeded. I was good at getting what I wanted. All the sisters hated me for it. Next day at school I saw Tanja and Caroline. They were so excited. They had the same shoes on. The green ones! My heart sank. I could have been part of this party of joy if I had the green shoes too. But I didn't, I wasn't. I wasn't part of the party. I had the blue shoes.

When I was seventeen or sixteen I started a stupid hobby. Paragliding. I did ask my parents because I needed a signature to do the introductory course. In Kössen, my home village, paragliding is very popular. The mountain is very suitable for it. When I was smaller, there was a world paragliding championship in my village. Organised by the guy who had a modern house in the village, actually, the only modern house in the village. He was married to an Australian woman which was unusual too. She always seemed to have a tan. The two kids were very different than the rest of us children, quiet and they spoke english. Outsiders. The older boy was in my younger sister's class. Two boys, Simon and Raoul, they also looked tanned all the time. The dad was Sepp Himberger. Some children from my school, I was one of them, we had to hold signs with names of the participating countries at the opening ceremony. I cannot remember who had China but they got lots of attention from all the Chinese participants. They went over to the child and took photos and they were laughing. I was jealous. I had San Marino, yeah. I have never even heard of this place. Was that really a country? Some sort of mistake. I stood there for the entire time. All alone, nobody came to me where all the other kids had someone coming over saying hello or taking photos and filming. I felt stupid with that stupid non existent country. Fifteen years later, when I finished at the Slade, I got curated into a big deal group show. Everybody else who exhibited in it did quite well in their professional lives. Everybody went on to have more exhibitions and they are mostly successful artists now. Everyone but me. Anyway, it was in San Marino. It really is a country. Very small.

Back to paragliding. My father said no and my mother was there too. He said I was too small and I was not allowed. I didn't mind too much because I knew my mum would sign it. She let us do everything we wanted. I thought I should at least ask my father. Usually we wouldn't even do that because we already knew the answer, no.

So, I started paragliding secretly to hide it from my father which wasn't difficult. I did the course and then went paragliding. Lots of boys from the village did it but no girls.

I was the only one. I think that was the most appealing part of the entire enterprise. I wasn't at school in the village anymore and was not friends with any of the girls from my village. I did see the boys when going out to the pubs with my older sister Eveline. I was getting on well with them. None of the girls I knew were going out, I have no idea what they were doing. Having a boyfriend maybe. Seriously I had no idea. I never even saw Margit anymore, my neighbour. She might have been already working as waitress, just like her mum, and smoking loads of cigarettes.

I didn't really get a buzz out of being in the sky. It wasn't a passion just an activity. Some of the other flyers were real enthusiasts. I wasn't. The other boys went flying a lot, every spare minute. I didn't go flying much. Since I finished my course I had been three or four times from the top of that mountain, the one I used to ski on in winter and everything was fine. It was a bit scary. My grandmother might have been suspicious. I don't know. I didn't have the impression she knew but she might have. One of the landing fields was right behind our house which would have been very convenient but grandma might have seen me landing when she was out in the garden and she would have told my father. That would have been awkward. She used to like chatting to anyone landing there so it was not an option for me.

It was a windy day. There were tons of paragliders up in the sky. Very busy. Alex, a neighbour lent me a special machine, some kind of wind detection machine. It would tell me when I was in a special wind area where if I turned a sharp corner I would twist up and up into the sky. It was pretty exciting when I was up so high, much higher than usual, for much longer than the other times were I basically jumped from the hill and slowly went down to the ground. I didn't want to go too high. I have heard stories where the paraglider gets sucked up into a cloud. That's bad. After a while I decided it was time to descend. I saw the landing field. Everything was as normal. At one edge of the field there was a little river. I always thought to myself, you don't wanna land in there... more scary stories. I went to make a simple turn by pulling down one of the handles and that was it.

They later told me I was up about ten meters, I turned the wrong way or the wind changed just as I turned, maybe I pulled the handle to fast, like I did up high just before with the strong winds. My paraglider collapsed on one side, all the air rushed out.

There was a hole in the grass from where my feet went into the ground. They said that.

The thing I remember was me saying: "Don't tell my dad!" and I remember people around me. I was totally out of it. I had no pain. I remember people talking, the ambulance people, and I remember the noise of the helicopter I was in. They took me to the closest town, St. Johann. I broke both my ankles and my back just a tiny bit, a hairline fracture. The doctors had to look three times to find that tiny fracture. I kept telling them it hurt, my back. My feet were an obvious disaster. I had lots of metal screws in them and I had to practise moving them which was difficult. My big toe on the left foot didn't do what I said anymore. I had to attach a string to it and pull it up, keep trying to move it.

25

It's still weird today that toe.

I was in hospital for weeks and had to get used to pooing into a bed pan. I just couldn't do it. It was so embarrassing, far too embarrassing. Every second or third day I had to take a suppository. That was compulsory for patients with this problem. Over time I slowly lost my inhibitions. I got a visit from a friend, Bounty. That was his nickname and he liked me. I had just peed into the pan and I lay on it for the entire visit just waiting for him to leave soon. I didn't want to call the nurse to take it out in front of him. After a few weeks the doctors decided to get me a cast for my torso so I could go home for a while. Getting that was painful. I had to pull myself up on a metal triangular frame so that my back was nicely stretched out. It really hurt and made me dizzy, I saw diamonds. I looked like a bug with this hard carapace around my body. I was driven home in the ambulance. It was a sunny day and there were flowers everywhere in the fields. The landscape had changed since I last saw it. Back at home in a wheelchair. That causes problems, being in a wheelchair. Just doing normal things like going to the toilet or getting dressed was a challenge, getting water from a very high sink in an industrial kitchen. It was in the afternoon. My mother and sisters all had plans to go out and were about to leave the house. I wanted to get water but I couldn't reach it. That moment I had a break down. Everybody was getting on with their lives and I was suspended in Limbo land. I started howling like a wolf, tears coming down in floods. I couldn't do any of the things everybody else could do. They still had a life, I didn't. That's the only time my sister Johanna ever felt sorry for me and cried too. It really had an effect on her but not enough of one to actually like me. She was always the biggest problem for me. I am scared of her.

I had to go back to hospital. They took off the cast and I had to stay. Back to bed. I wasn't looking forward to the toilet business again, but surprisingly that wasn't a problem anymore and I was almost healed and functioning quite well so it was a piece of cake and not long before I was discharged.

My father never came to see me in hospital. I was always convinced it was because deep down he is too sensitive to see his daughter like this and he would have to cry. I had phantasies about my father being very kind and caring. He just couldn't show it. Realistically, he was probably just angry or not interested. He did say NO to paragliding after all. All his orders were always ignored from all of us girls. It's quite depressing really. There was no reasoning and no talking either. It's possible he just didn't want to be involved raising children. How would I know. As I said, nobody every talked about feelings or desires. I really have no idea what is going on in my family, something disturbed. My two younger sisters, Johanna and Edith came only once, one time and they looked like they were forced to come. My older sister came once, maybe? My mother and my sister Regina came to see me every single day. One day my mother and the other day Regina.

I was already eighteen years old then or nineteen, I know because that's when I lost my car to Regina. She was eighteen too by now and got to drive my old car which was our parent's old car. I was obviously not using it. My school class went on a trip to the Hebrides. I missed that too unfortunately. My teacher, Susanna Hanl, bought me a lot of books to read. She was really nice to me, thinking about it. My two friends at school always made fun of her. Especially my best friend Sylvia. She could be very mean. I am not friends with her any more. She made fun of Miss Hanl carrying lots of folders, up to her chin. I remember her, the teacher, saying in a husky, quiet complaining voice, "Please,... be quiet, I have a headache." Maybe she was a bit weird.

This was not the done thing in my school but some students for some reason thought it was worthwhile and they got excited about it and made a half decent year book. I was depicted with a carrot in my hand. Extremely boring and healthy, I know, and it was true too. I really was on a health trip in my past because I once read a book about the dangers of white sugar and white flour or something like that. When we were on a school trip to Prague I was dreading the visits to McDonalds and I would always get the salad. I think the actual lives of people are actually really boring most of the time, not just mine but also Beyonce's and Kendall Jenner's. I just saw Christmas shots of them made by themselves and their lives look just like everybody else's to me. It's only the professional look and shots and videos that give the illusion of it being different and special. But it's not.

The diamonds are like bricks filling a window. From the outside you cannot really make out what is going on but from the inside it's a big mountain of bricks laying all over the place. It is a beautiful loft. Huge windows with streaming sunlight. It warms the skin. Old windows, they are a bit cloudy, murky. Beautiful wooden slats on the floors. Oldish looking dirty white walls. The ideal artist's loft. Now I just need to fill it with a couch and a desk and all my artist's materials. And get rid of the bricks. It's in New York of course. I have never been to New York. Is it cold or is it hot? The Austrian mountain girl in the big city. Yodel ay he ho! Let's get Chinese take out. I am still no good with the sticks but it's not too bad. It gets delivered in those little white paper boxes. Sitting on the floor on a mattress. An imaginary mattress. Wouldn't it be good? We'd sit and laugh. What amazing times. Get to stay in New York and in a massive space. It's the golden times. The children come running in. The nanny brought them up, of course, all three of them. The oldest is Jack ten, second one, the disabled Eve, nine. She is kind of autistic and cannot do a million things and she is getting bigger now. And the little whirlwind Tasmanian devil who says 'no' all the time, Rocky. He is three and a real honest to gods handful. They all sit down and get snacks. Sausages and fruit and biscuits. They don't like Chinese take out. Now it's a family. Orestes and Diamond have lost their youths. The three persons who make spontaneity impossible are sitting there just like the bricks next to them. It's a heavy baggage. Lots of great stuff too, of course. Sure, lots of great stuff. And mountains of bricks.

We, us two are walking. The three in tow. It's five. five. five diamonds an understandable but incomprehensible woe. Who knows how this all happened and where did the spontaneity go? How can you understand, is the world still turning, how can you be free if you are carrying bricks around. Is it good, is it worth it? It's great to have little humans. little humans. big humans. the little ones are fun. they are not finished yet they have to become persons. and everybody becomes a different person. so much struggle. so much trying to find things. it's never ending. and the diamonds in the pockets, lugging them around. trying to have both things in my life, diamonds and bricks. the important thing that makes me a person. my own person. not defined by trying to make the little ones persons. they do it themselves but they need grown ups to look after them. they really do. this takes time. split. a big split of split interest. the family. they, the family. which way is it going. strong hold. families are weird things. all kinds of different things happen to all those families. all types of different things happen to all kinds of humans. How varied. How similar.

Sitting in the garden in the Hamburg fancy hotel one summer. I work here, it's my break and it's a sunny day in the big city far away from my home village. Far up high a bird sings and then something lands right on the front of my white work shirt. I know that means good luck but the stain is hard to get out especially when you try to scrub it off with toilet paper in the bathroom while still wearing the shirt. Me, the waitress, fantastic waitress, such a brilliant waitress. I wait all my life, get food from the kitchen and bring it over. Everything always tastes wonderful, they never wait too long and they just love it, getting waited on, getting sustenance, the people. Never any problems, everything smooth and beautiful. My mother's hotel was just like that. Brilliant. We all, the entire family, made sure the food went out and it was all good. No uncooked fish drama in the main hall and people screaming for food with angry red faces. Total chaos, a man over there chucking his cutlery right in the face of his neighbour and he is bleeding and screaming and attacking him back with his fork. Not like that.

And then I run downstairs to the one million year old cellar to escape it all. The walls are black and uneven, this black hole called cellar looks like it might have been carved out from a rock formation, this is the foundation of the inn. A hallway with rooms coming off it, one for fruit and vegetables in crates, one for heating, one has two washing machines in it and there is a fridge room and two freezers in another room also with bottles and massive jars of home cooked jams stored behind wooden slats, it's locked but you can see in between the slats. Not sure why the jams need to be locked away. They need to have a space somewhere. I hide for a bit in the cool and dark with the freezers. I get out my paper and pen and draw some diamonds. It's soothing, it calms. No story in that picture or representation but the image freezes a static moment in time. There is no movement back or forth. There is only a little nudge from the irregularities of hand drawn shapes. Human error. No perfection. Nobody is perfect. Nobody is better. I like the way the field of shapes looks. So plain. No story to tell, numb, quiet. The crouching tiger is sitting in the corner, pad on lap, graphite in hand. But the shapes, cool.

The craziness continues upstairs, my parents wondering where I was. I, running out of time, have to face the lion soon. Trying to make people happy. Really? Is that possible? I am still deluded after all this time. So much water has come down this river and I have not learnt anything. Know thyself they say. I am not sure if I am brave enough, a sad little creature.

Delivering fresh hot bad childhoods. Have I destroyed my

boy's childhood? No kids around him ever. No interaction and always isolation. Suspended hanging, instability. No equipment to be the good mother. I have made mistakes and impacted another person's life negatively. I have not equipped him well, to be able to lead a happy and fulfilled life with other people in it. The only thing I did was counting from one to ten each time I changed his nappy. I had no words, no songs, I should not have even been allowed to be a parent. Who gave permission? Is this like killing a person? It's probably worse because I cause life long suffering.

I have no idea what I did wrong with my second delivery. Probably everything right from the beginning. We can see how she would be if she was healthy. If. If she didn't have all those missing genes, them missing destroys her ability to do a simple thing like talk or run. Lots of hitting and screeching because I can't give her what she wants and needs and because I am happy to dump her in front of the TV all day so she doesn't bother me, so she seems happy.

The littlest one, another boy, is a different story again. I took him to be around children from when he was six months old. Seven years after his older brother was born life has changed and we live in a different country and in different circumstances and everybody and everything has changed. We are older. He talks a lot and is funny. But he is a time-bomb. I am scared of his flip outs. He becomes a terror machine at the drop of a hat. He is only three and he only ever says no, always and every time he says, no! Never yes to anything. I have to be so careful not to upset him, walking on glass. It's so difficult. He went to school since the age of two. Probably I did the other extreme of putting him away too early instead of too late. See, everything goes wrong. All the other families are so perfect and happy. There are some good moments sometimes too.

Diamonds diamonds diamond fairy cake. diamond lady. Diamond Frances. diamonds in the trees and diamonds in the oven, diamonds in your tea and on the chair. diamonds in your bed and in your slippers. in the sky and on the sea. on the mountain and in church. the rabbit has diamond ears. diamonds on the horse too. diamonds in the grass and in the autumn leaves. diamonds in the sky. sparkly sounds and sparkly eyes and hair. the diamond party begins and there will by fairy cakes diamond fairy cakes and diamond bunting in black and diamond confetti and everybody has to come with diamond clothing. There'll be diamond ice cubes in diamond cocktails and music. Lots and lots of amazing and wonderful interesting fun diamond people. All my friends and acquaintances are coming to Diamond Frances's party. Even the press is trying to get in. They'll get 20 minutes in an hours time. But then they'll really have to go again. Sorry. The photos look so staged. Standing around with a drink in your hand chatting, posing, laughing. It's so done, so usual, so every Saturday, it's a bit weird. A Party?

I once had a party. sixteen? maybe. Shame I only invited a few people from my school in St. Johann. It was the next town and all the girls came from different villages. None from my village. If I would have simply invited more people from my village I would have been more successful, I think. I didn't want to have a party with the people I used to go to primary school with, it was that simple. I didn't see them as part of my life. The girls in my school weren't part of my life either, really. Just a little cooler, or a lot. So I ended up, naturally, with not much of a party, not much of anything. I had two party guests. Hermann and Christina. She was the farmer's daughter and lived two minutes away and Hermann was her boyfriend. Embarrassing really. Nobody turning up would have been better. I know why they were there though, they lived close... They were there together. He got cavalier and went into the village centre trying to invite some people, round them up. And then some of the boys I went to school with turned up. I think that was better than nobody. They were actually quite fun and I did know them from going out in the village. Future farmers and carpenters mainly. I don't know what the girls did, what became of them. The ones I went to primary school with. They never went out, I never saw them and have never seen any of them again. No idea. Not that I missed them then, or now. After that party I had another one or perhaps two in my whole life. Maybe three in total. I am not big on parties. Really not big on parties. I'm not a party-girl. I am more into diamonds I guess. At least it's more my thing. Less negative outcomes. Negative outcome. negative outcome. my diamonds will conquer the world. I won't be a negative outcome anymore. Everybody will love them and everybody will love me because they love my diamonds and all my friends will invite me to fairy-cake parties and I can bring the diamonds. for everybody to pin onto their faces. It will be so much fun and I really cannot wait.

Diamond used to have a different name. She comes from the Austrian mountains. She was born on an actual mountain. Her mother never wanted her. There was only supposed to be one girl, the first. Not more. But each time the father came home from working on the ships, the mother got pregnant again, and each time it was another girl. Five times. Diamond was the second girl closely followed by the third one who was premature. Another two girls followed after that but there was a bit of a gap after the third and there was definitely a deep split between the older and the younger groups of sisters. The younger ones, their lives were totally different. There was the time before the hotel came into the family and the time after the hotel which caused a slow glacial family breakdown. The father had to come home from the ships permanently after number four was born because there were too many obligations with all those children and the business. There were three grandmothers, two grandmothers and one great grandmother, and no grandfathers at all. One had moved away to Vienna and the other two were dead in the ground. A house full of women. five girls, one mother, three grandmothers (only one lived in the same house) and just one father. This lone male was marginalised and slowly stripped of all influence and power, castrated and turned into furniture. He was grumpy and forced to lead his own life but it occupied the same space.

As soon as there was any chance of leaving that place, Diamond took it.

It was part of her education to get work experience over the summer months. She started off working in a different little village in Austria. The next summer she was a nanny in the Parisian suburbs with lots of travelling all over France and a summer in Hamburg in Germany. One summer at home because of broken legs and back and then to London, as soon as school was finished. Never to return. Always away.

The grandmother was sad. She was the father's mother. She was always nice to Diamond but mean to pretty much everybody else especially to the daughter-in-law, Diamond's mother. It was quite poisonous atmosphere but not always and really only generally, vaguely.

Diamond does not have any contact with her family now, she is estranged and tries hard to get her own life together. She is still struggling being a grown up and looking after herself by earning money. She has never conformed to normal standards of getting a job and earning money. Sometimes she did. But she could never identify with her profession. It was always something alien to her. Until she realised she wanted to be an artist but she is not a good businesswoman or good socially, where she is really very bad. In fact, I think not a soul likes her. She used to have friends earlier but thought they weren't really good friends. They have disappointed her and she just let them go. too idealistic. Now she is hiding in a cave, she draws diamonds only and makes her own clothes. She has succumb to total social and financial alienation.

My love story.

It was at an art exhibition of a sort of friend acquaintance. He stood over there, tall with slacks, that's the word he uses for trousers, the converse trainers, button up shirt, hanging out and a grey suit jacket with round Ramones pins on the lapel. Very cool but also not really. He was all alone and I saw straight through him. It was like I knew that person. So fragile, when I touch it it breaks into a million pieces. Lonely and sad. I was hooked. When he turned up my day suddenly became timeless. I felt like not such an outsider. Unwanted item. I was happy.

I look out of my window and there they are, there he is. He looks up, waves and smiles. He is the only one to notice me. The only one who matters. I wave and smile back. I am happy.

Going out together into the night. He is wearing a white jacket and I wear something weird and handmade. I embarrass myself dancing like a crazy person. The people there at the event are still talking about it today. I have no idea what he thinks, I am delirious and don't care. Walking along the streets of London, to some other place, I feel like a princess.

Later, when I wash his clothes, the old off white shirts with faint diamond patterning, they must have been washed a million times, soft and the boxer shorts too. Faint diamond pattern in white, off white with other colours faint. I hang them on my old second hand washing rail which is probably as old as these shirts. It's red and I still have it. I loved doing it, hanging up those clothes. He is not there but his clothes are.

The engagement ring. It was not romantic because it was planned because of other more practical reasons and it was in the kitchen. In Switzerland. Yeah, Switzerland. How the heck did we end up there anyway? But it was romantic. He knew I would say yes. It was just a formality. But still he was nervous. So sweet. Just perfect. I said yes. I still have the ring.

We bought rings from a department store. Wedding rings. On the ground floor. Fake jewellery. A tenner maybe for both. I put it on and was freaking out. Almost couldn't get it off. Was I there with him or alone? I cannot remember. How would I know the size. I think I was there alone. They lasted for a month after our wedding. We don't have wedding rings. We never got new ones.

Does he love me? I would like that. I am so lucky he puts up with me because I am such a selfish bitch sometimes. We are like two peas in a pod, so similar and so different at the same time. and we have a lovely family too. three kids.

That's what I like about children. They love you back. Unconditionally. At the beginning anyway. That is selfish but I like it, the guarantee of love. Someone I can be sure loves me and who wants my love back. It can be a shock when you realise one day that the people you thought loved you don't even like you. Bad feeling, bad feelings. Like my mother. It's possible she hates me. I don't like her either. I just assumed I was loved, I thought you get love automatically if you are in a certain situation, like a family or a relationship. I still don't know how it works.

He can be so annoying though. I am getting used to it, mundane annoyance. Especially giving birth. I want to just lie there and make groaning and moaning noises, given up to pain. And he wants me to snap out of it. Snap out of it? Crazy and totally unreasonable.

We lived close enough to walk to the hospital. It was in the morning, busy Berlin Kreuzberg. All the school kids we passed were indifferent to my tragedy, maybe a woman or two saw the pain in my face feeling sorry for me and knowing it themselves. Walking, in labour, to the hospital! It's what the midwifes said is good. Women come to hospital way too early… I can't walk anymore. As soon as we are on the hospital grounds I refuse to walk another step and grab hold of some metal rail and hang on for my life. He runs inside and comes back with a wheelchair. I am feeling safe now. But there is more to come.

He is smart and unfortunately right a lot of the time. He loves that, for some reason, being right. It's good to have an intelligent husband. I like having a smart husband. But not always, as in really always, and I have to make sure I still think about things for myself. I have to remember to separate myself from him. I need to make decisions. He lets me decide things, he forces me to do so in a way. It's important to take responsibility, but I was never good at it. I used to blame him for every single mistake we made, lots of those. He won't let that happen anymore. I like growing up with him. Together we age.

And he always wears sunglasses, white rimmed sunglasses. Even in winter.

◆

Diamond has decided she just does things for her own interest now. Everybody is out of her view, she has made a border for not getting hurt. She is immune against rejection, dejection, irrelevancy and decided to make her own world. She has decided to make her own legacy, a body of work, her body of work, stored in this cave until somebody or nobody ever finds it. It doesn't matter. It's what she does it is her world. She is building her own world and living in it too. Lucky there are a handful of people who look after her. Bring her food and sometimes talk to her. She is like a shy fox and scared. But she is great, she perseveres and will be triumphant over society. She has not bent down to foolery and falseness. She is now who she always was but more crystallised, more diamond like. Pure diamond. The hardest thing in the world.

From now on I will always say the truth, no more lying or not saying anything. There is always something to talk about, isn't there? Where have all the bugs gone? There is not a single one in the kitchen. Who has taken my toaster? There was still so much bread in here and I wanted to eat it all. I have diamond jam. Greengages cut into diamond shapes. My great grandma had a tree, a greengage tree and also a cherry one but she never had many cherries. I cannot remember the cherries much. The birds ate them. But there were so many greengages. I loved them. Like little plums, round ones, not oval, with yellowish green very thin skin and flesh. The flesh is soft and very juicy and there is a stone. There was lots and lots of jam. But all the stones were in it so you had to take out the stones, fish them off the bread with your finger before you start eating or take them out of your mouth. I didn't do that. Only if there was a greengage stone hiding in the jam that I missed. It's the best jam that ever was.

Once when we went skiing in the middle of winter just after Christmas I perceived a big big black shape at the top of the mountain. I was overcome with the desire to roll it down, to get it rolling but it wasn't moving. That's when I decided, I will do this for the rest of my life. I will make diamonds, draw them, in black and they will be colossal. My parents saw me trying to push the diamond shape off the mountain. I wanted it to turn into an avalanche and bring the entire village down. Destroy everything. I don't like the village. It stinks. It stinks all over Austria. That's why I left. I don't like it there. I know I am one of them. I don't like myself either. *Das Volk*. Uptight and mean. I feel it inside of me too. It's inside of me. I remember what I felt like when I went to stay with my parents on a holiday. I felt like I was the same as them. I miss that. A sense of belonging and sameness. Where all your history is engraved into your body. You are made of the same material. I don't have that anymore. I left them. I abandoned them because being there destroys important things inside me. They knock me down and then I have to collect all my pieces together and start from fresh. I would lose about three to four months of myself each time I went there and go once or twice a year. This meant kind of living in a void of no doing and just wallowing around, being destroyed back to nothing, to self-hate and pointlessness. Going backwards in a negative way. It's all over now. I think they are even happier without me than I am without them. I think I might have caused them anguish too. Me being there meant bad things for them too because of the difference that came with me. The threat of the big black shape. Not the sameness. The sameness is much less.

Diamond's daughter was born with a diamond head. There were so many tears. Everybody was crying. Even the doctors and nurses. The mother was taken away for surveillance. She was in great danger of dying. It was lucky that this was the half year they were staying in Paris. The second half is with the father, the goat shepherd from

Mongolia. The grandparents there would be even more outraged, eating their goat testicles. They would have thrown her over the cliffs as soon as she came out, there's no room for that there. Maybe not. Maybe people aren't that cruel. They get overwhelmed with incapacity. No idea how to act or react. She's a kid only, a little girl, and it's not right. Why us? Why us? What have we done to deserve this? Everybody else has healthy children. They are all running around doing children things, family things but the diamond headed cannot. They are excluded. Have to go for a different kind of life. Just has to be. Diamond headed daughter might end up being great at something or just a very loveable or loving person. Diamond head is precious and unique.

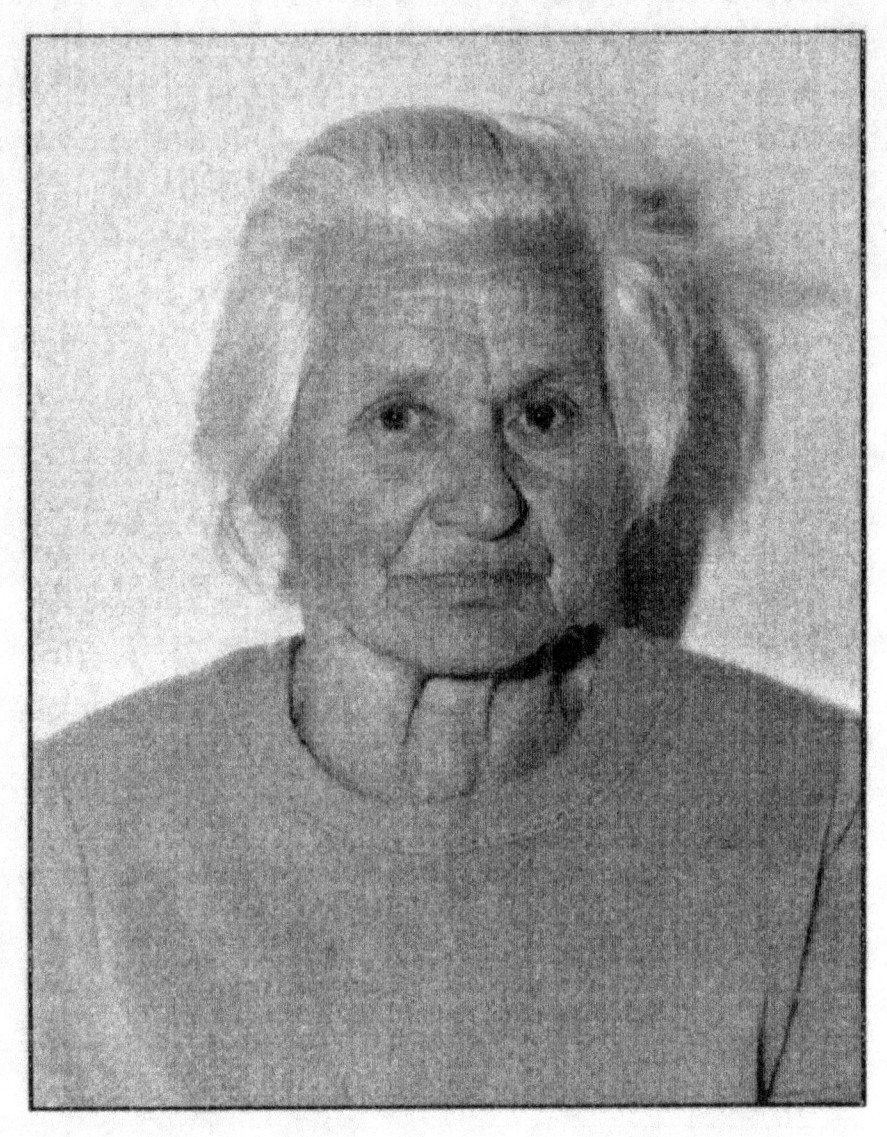

Arbeitsam und einfach war dein Leben,
treu und fleißig deine Hand,
Ruhe hat dir Gott gegeben,
rasten hast du nie gekannt.

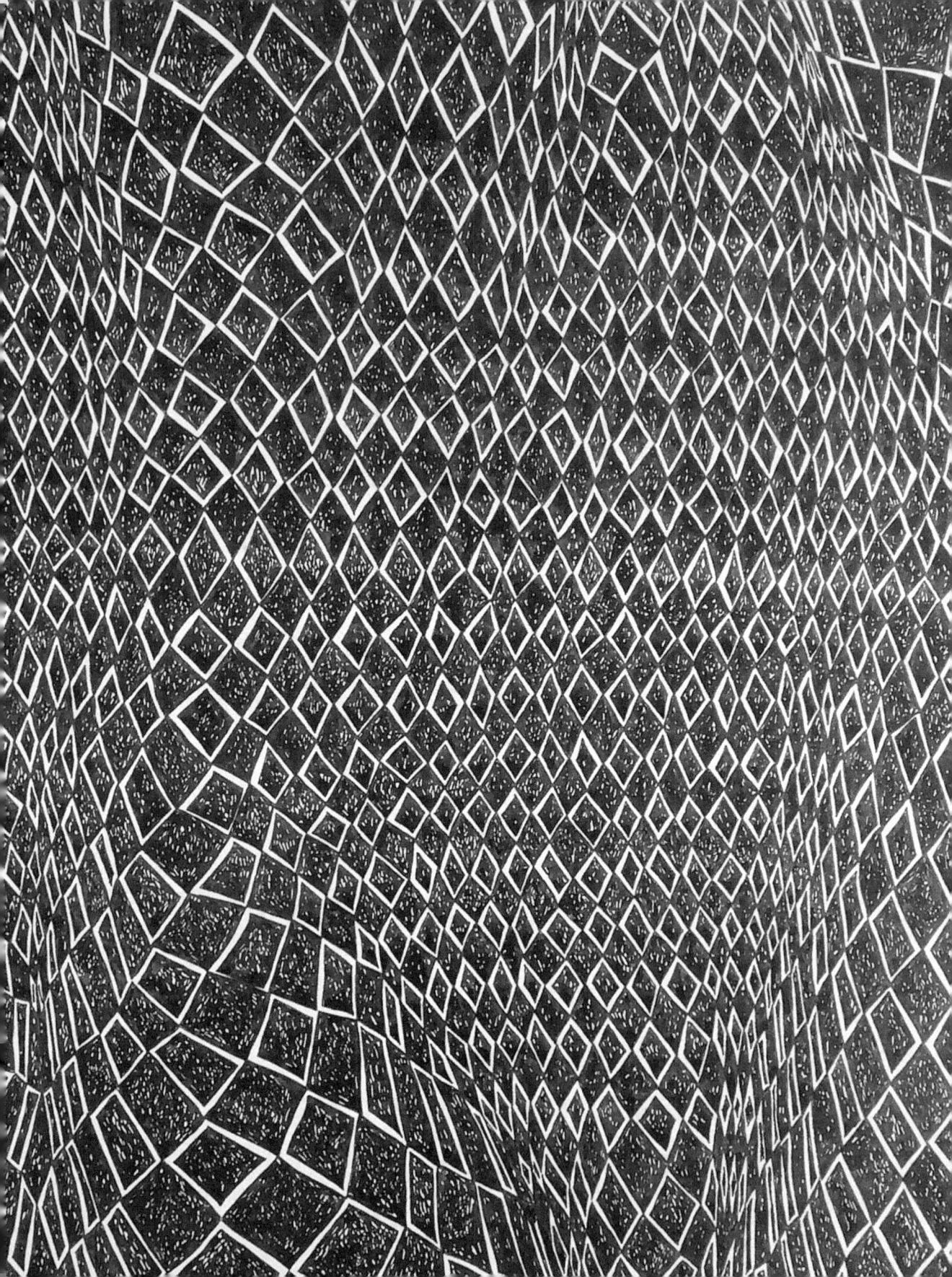

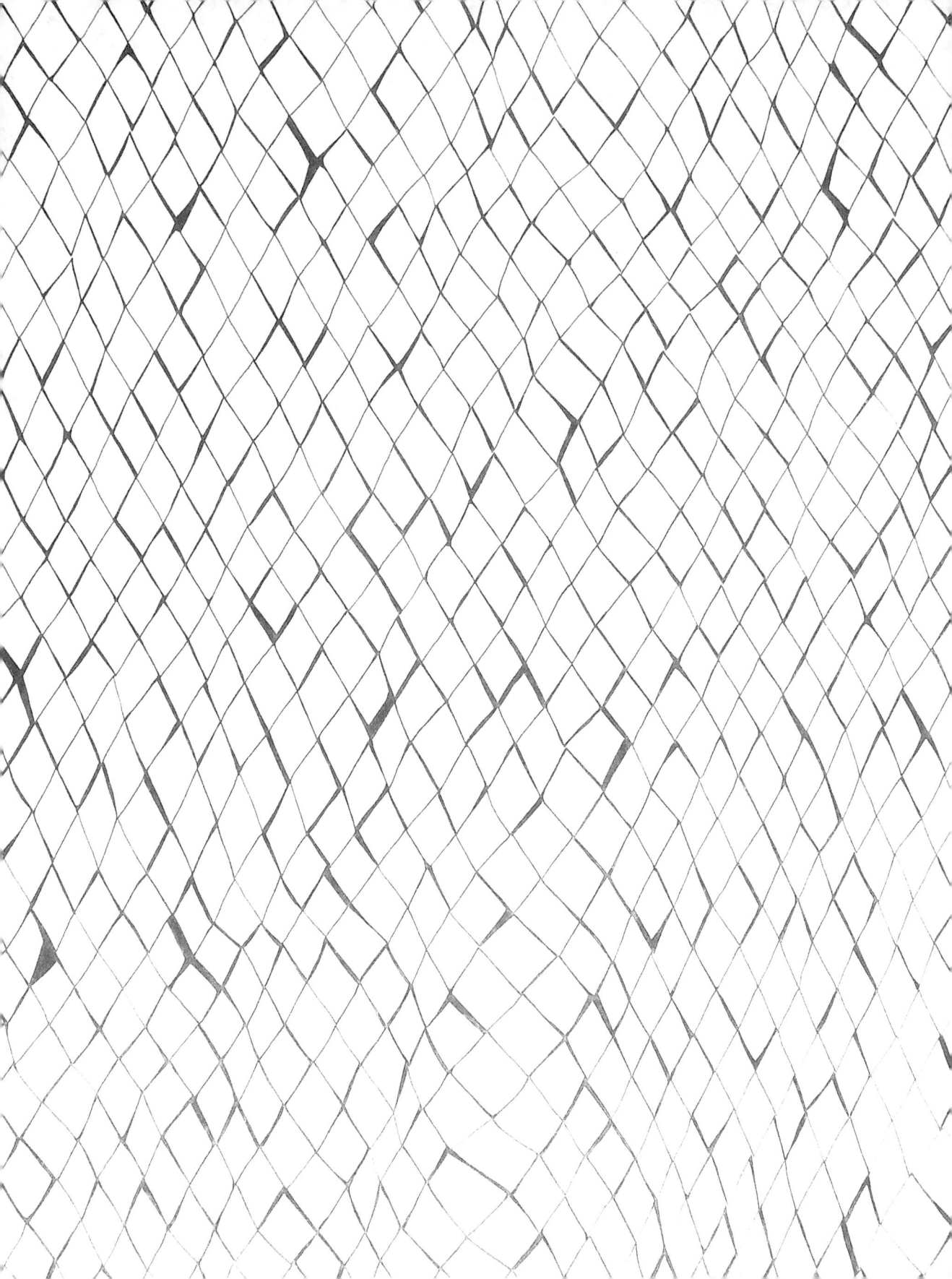

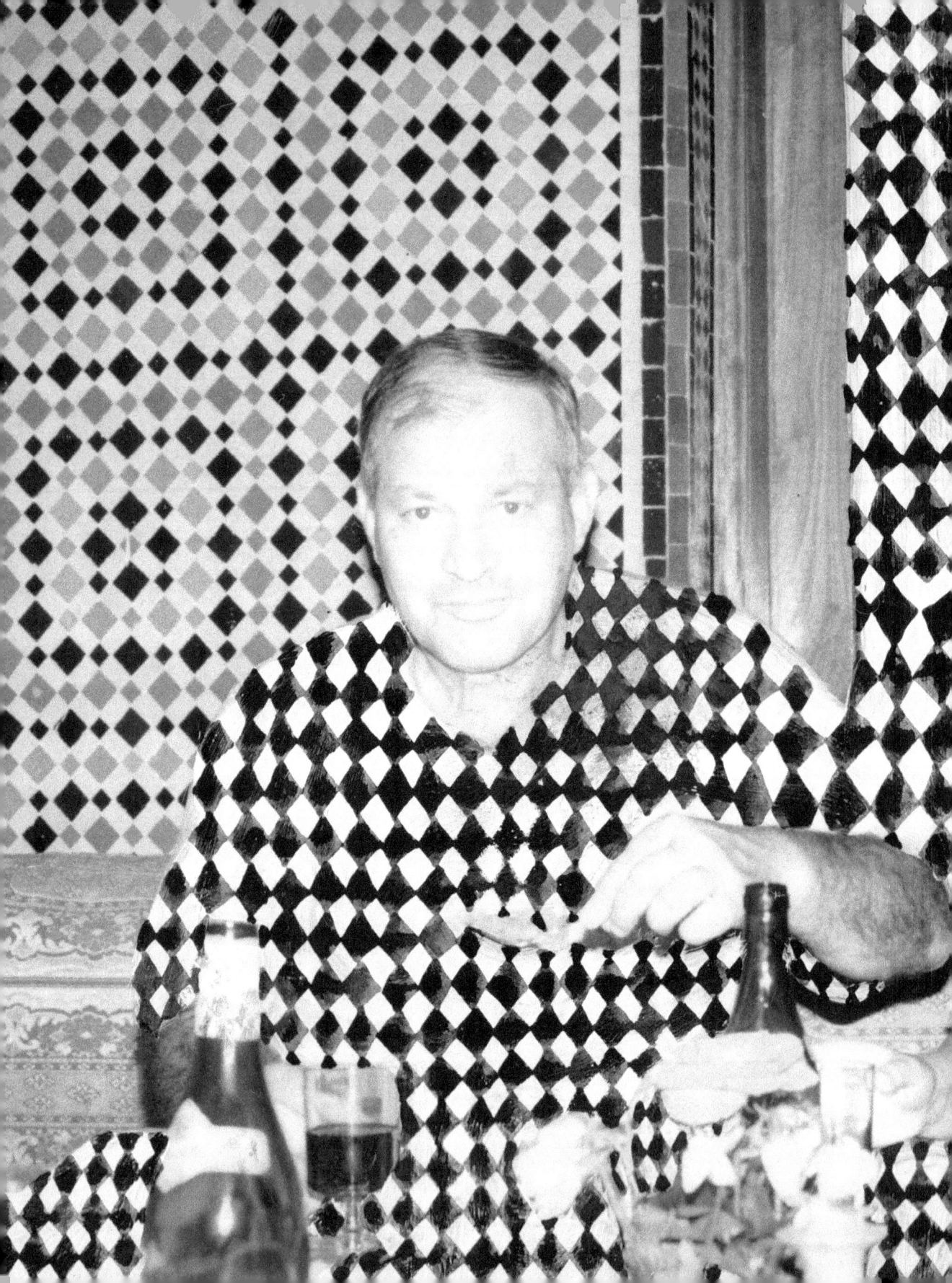

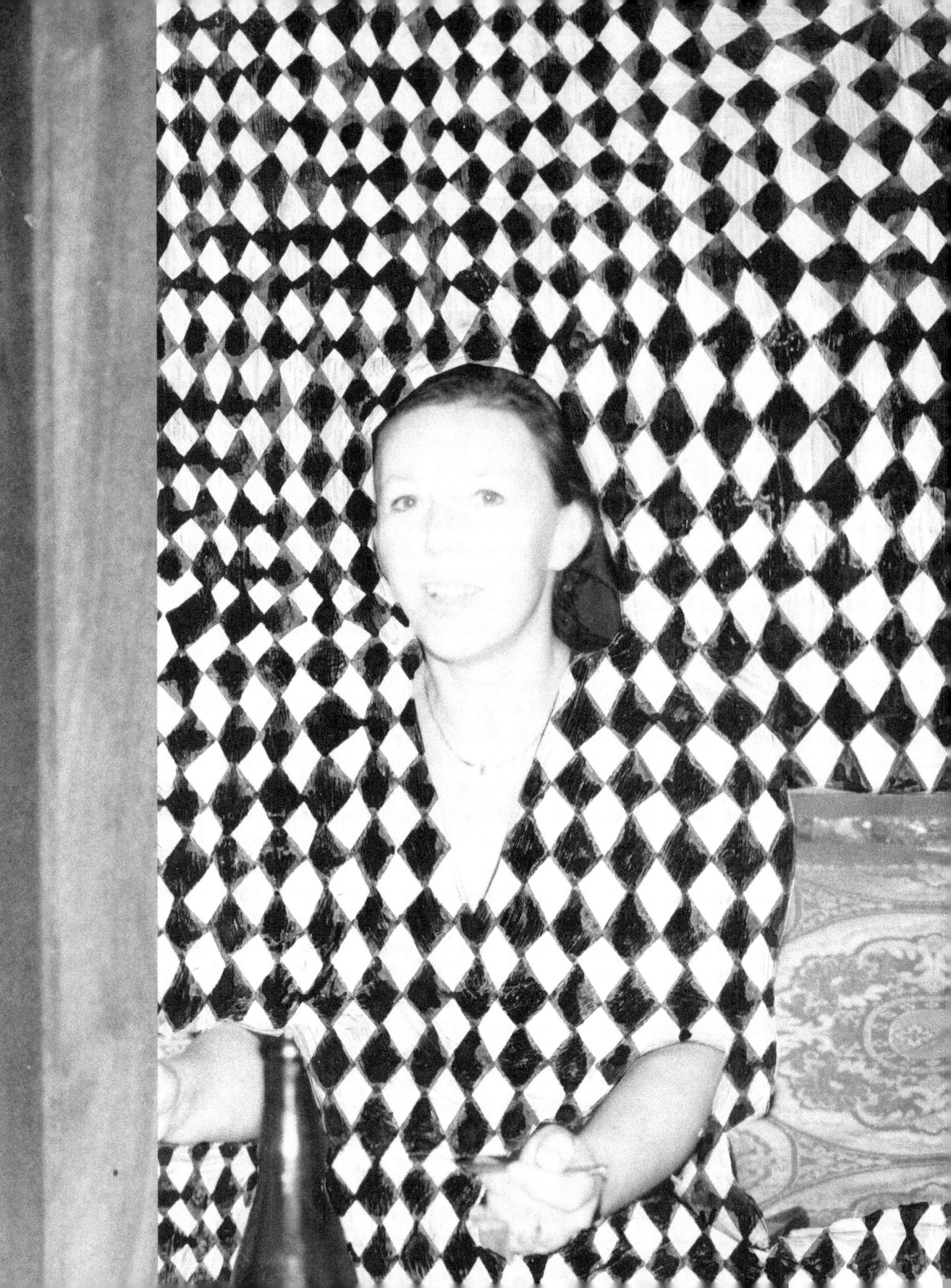

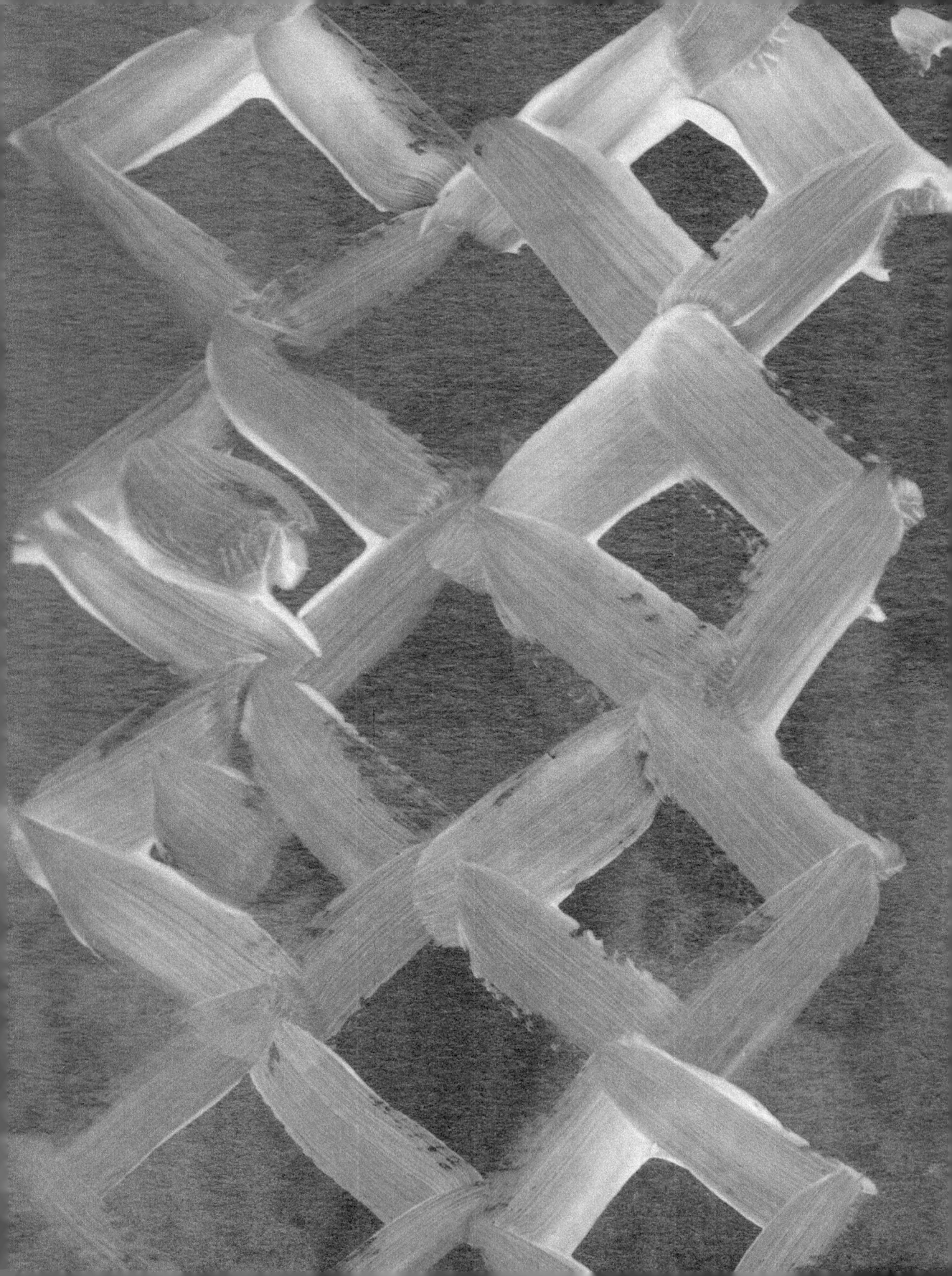

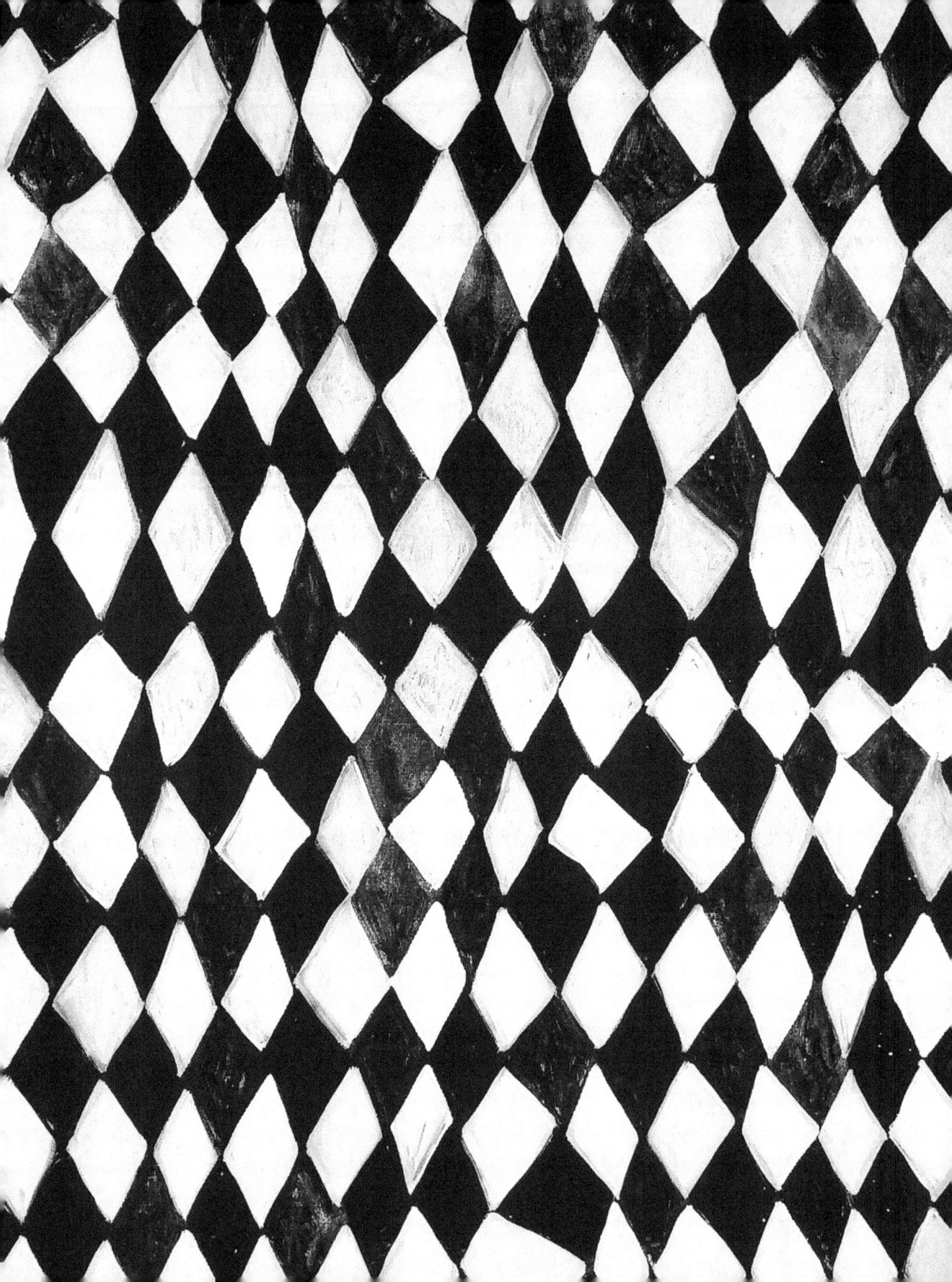

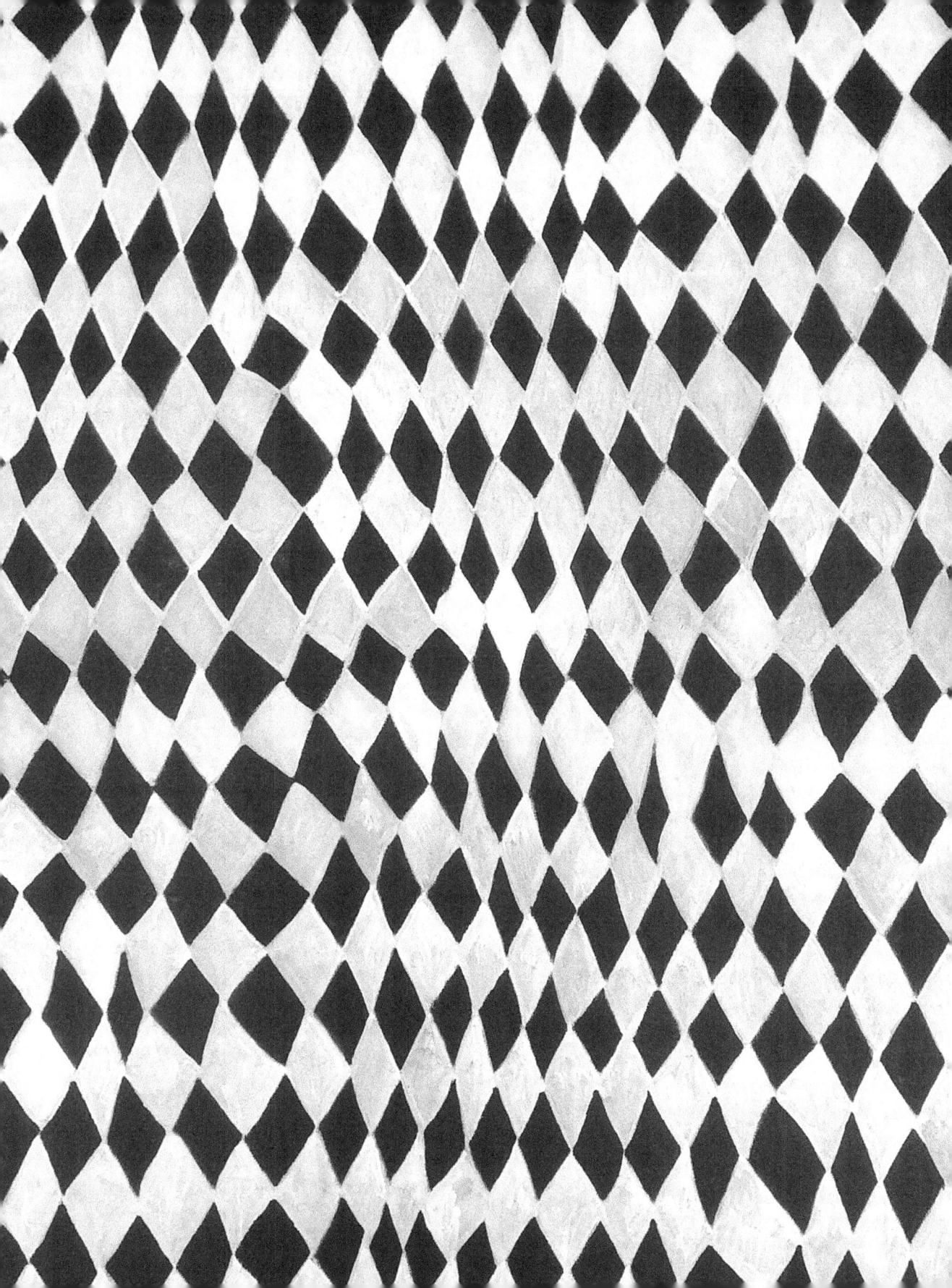

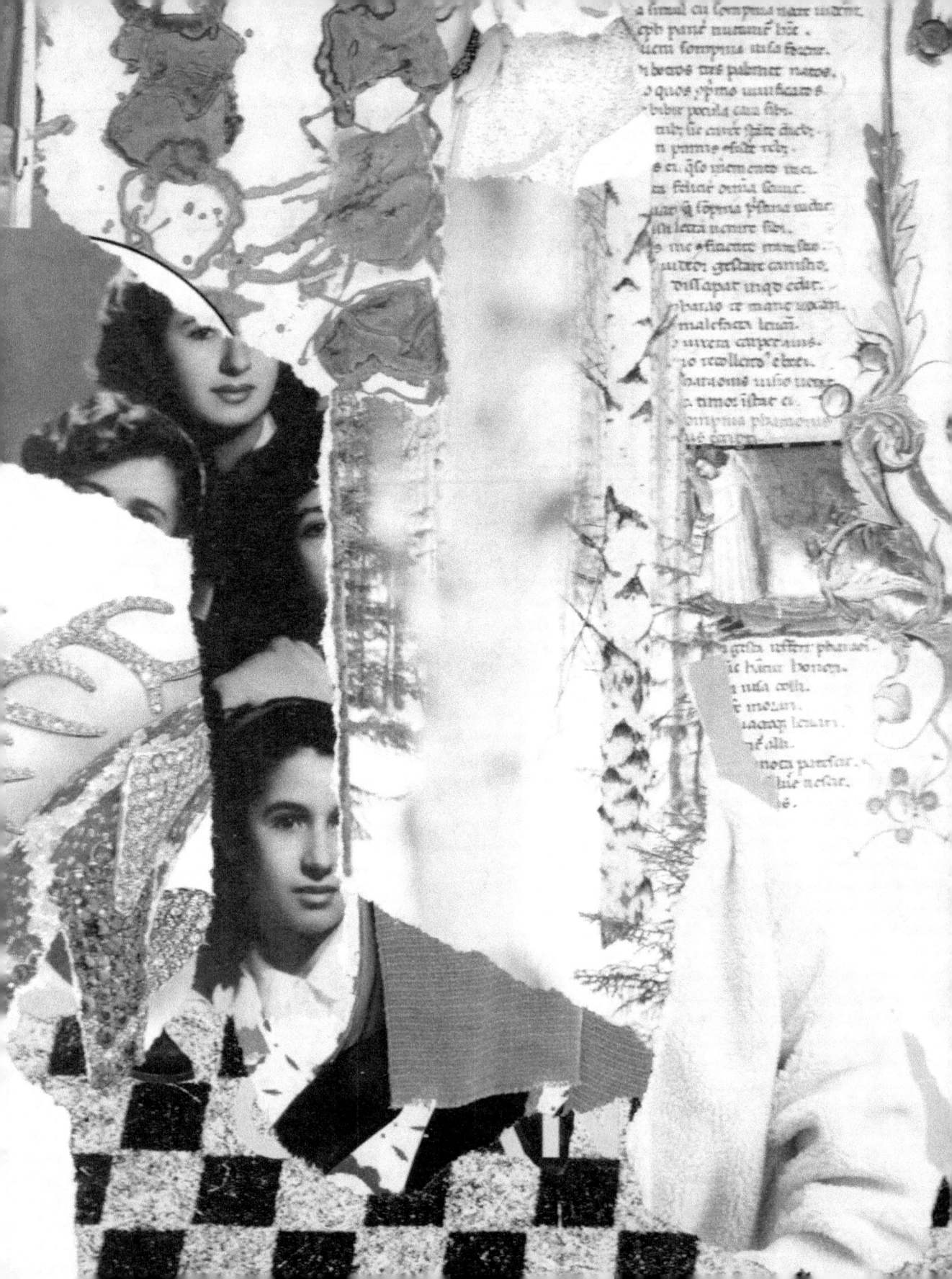

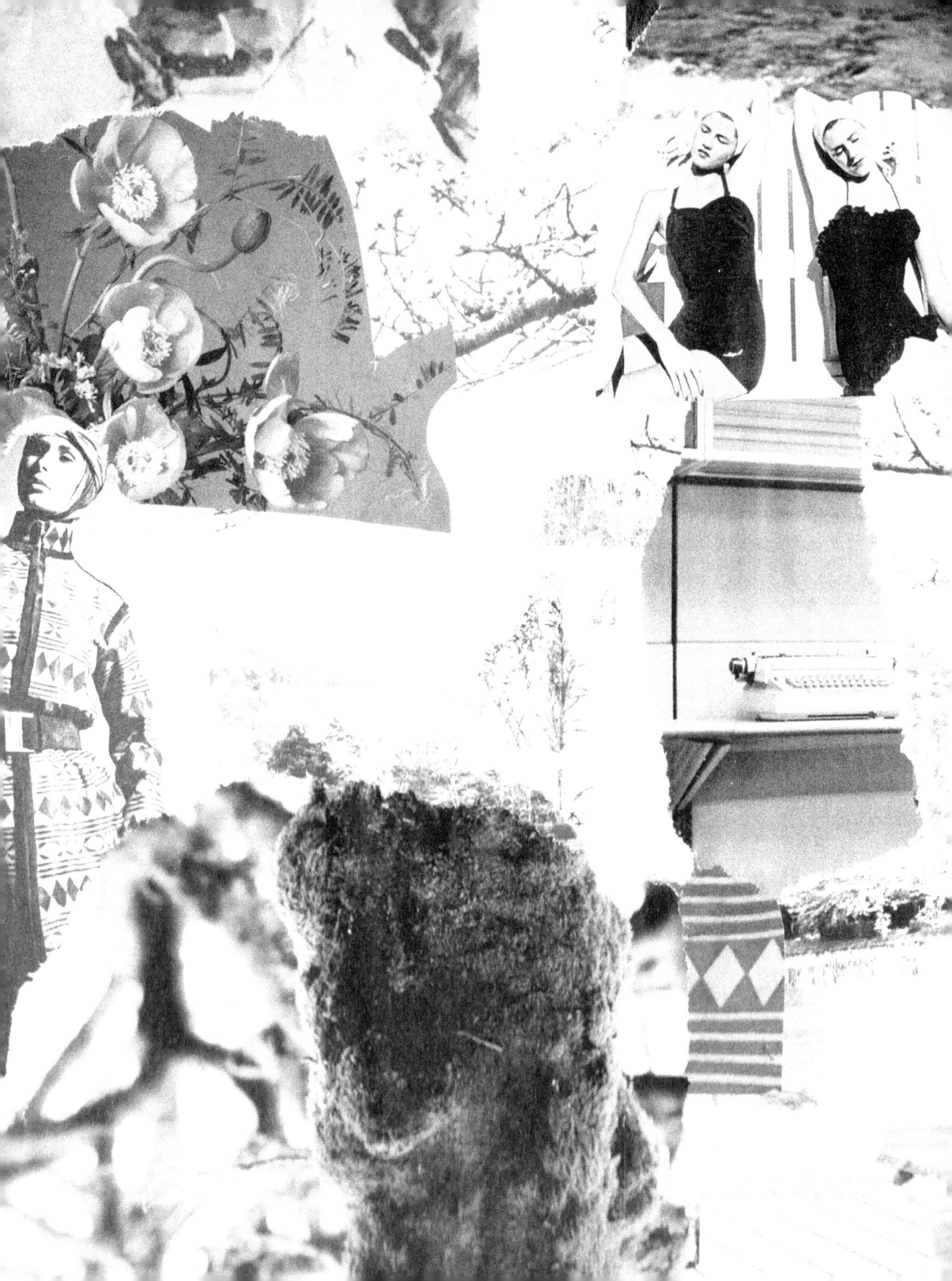

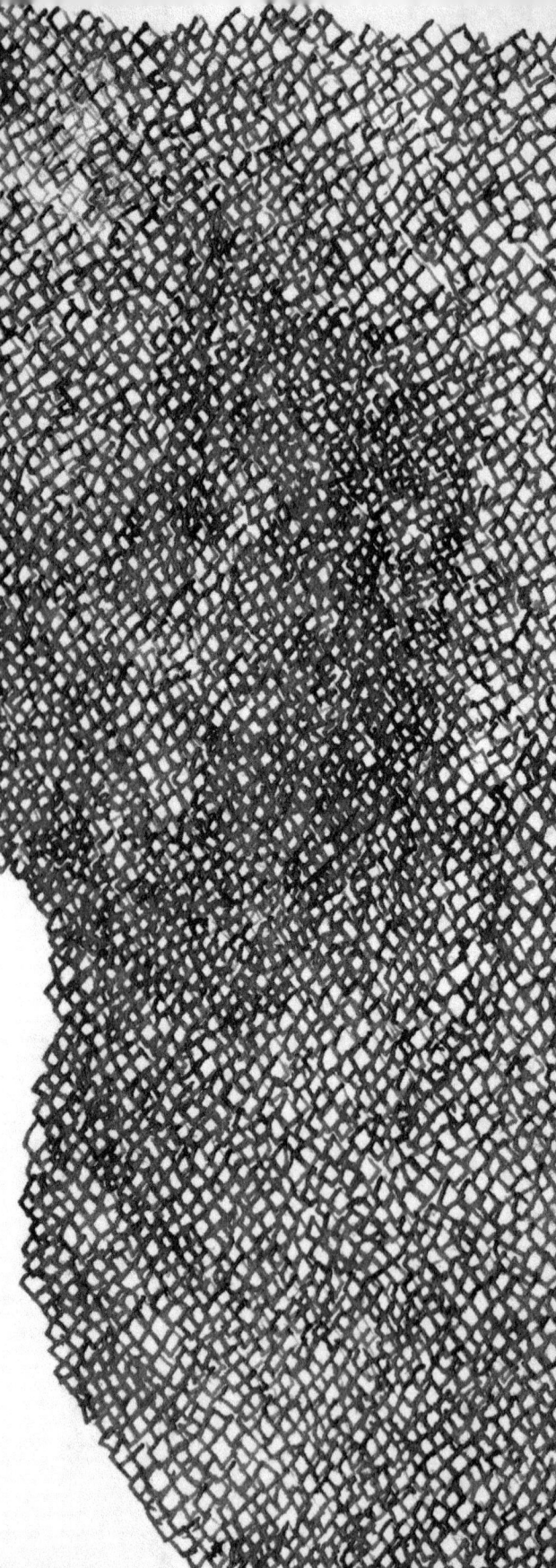

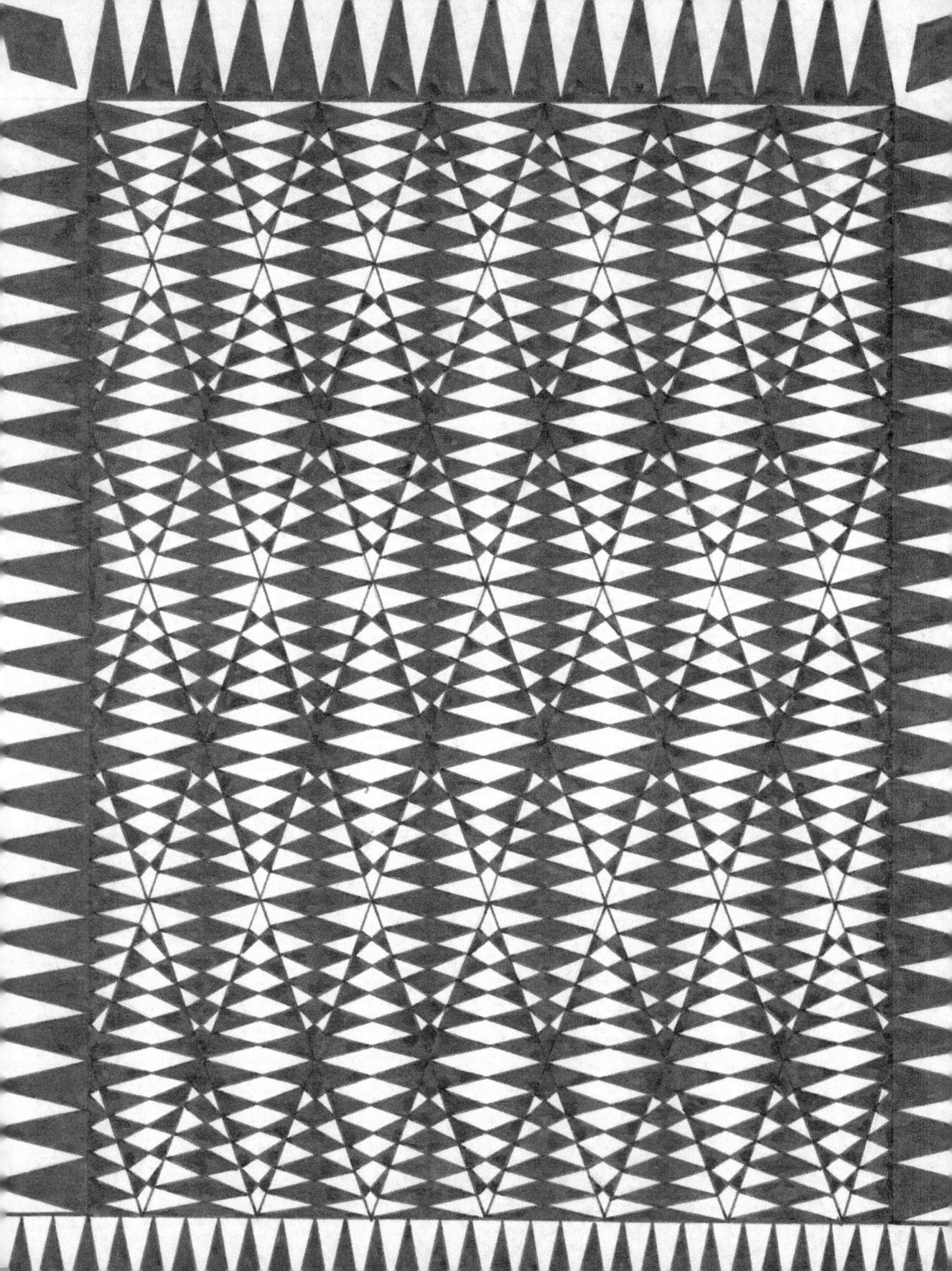

QUARRY

I am into world building. I make my very own world. A tinkling noise of diamonds suspended in a headpiece like Mongolian headdresses. I saw them on TV, very high up and hanging things that make a noise when she moves. I walk around with this tinkling noise. On my school run, sitting on the bus. In my normal life. Give it all a bit of a sparkle. And no one knows about it. It's personal. Diamonds are a shape. Picasso used this pattern in his pictures to show his presence, I think. A bit like Yayoi Kusama and her dots. Surroundings and clothes. I copy dots, diamonds, interchangeable. Agnes Martin is wearing a white diamond suit on one of the photos. She is still young there. It looks fantastic. She is doing her work.

I like dullness. I like boring. No movement, or very little. Nothing offensive, extremely offensive. I like extremely offensive. Fine. It's for me. Nobody is ever going to like this. Not even you can get excited about this. It's so nice not to have to decide, to deliberately and excruciatingly come up with oh so interesting, such enticing subject matter, excite the viewer. I am not playing the genius in the studio. So many painters doing their struggling and working hard on finding what the picture wants. 'It wasn't right and it needed something else.' Starting with a sketch and an idea and then changing until it's all just right. The eternal struggle and striving for truth. The truth of the world inside the painting. It's all bullshit. They pretend to be so important and assume to be transmitter of a heavenly communication. They can channel it. I am not doing that. I execute the painting. It's all already there and I am a person.

That gets everybody's blood going. I was never a virtuoso anyway. Never wanted to get better or be excellent. This is the ultimate faking, faking absence. Pretending to myself. Complete indulgence in self delusion and nobody is even laughing because nobody is looking.

But I will be a virtuoso anyway. I want to get better, be excellent, achieve excellence in my diamond production.

Real diamonds are so desirable. These ones are so undesirable. diamonds, diamonds.

I am looking forward to using colour. Maybe one day. It will be more varied but I am still into black right now. Especially because of the kind of crisis I am in. Denouncement. It took all those years to find out what I wanted to do because I needed to get older, more mature. It's about time. The diamonds represent time for me. The lozenge shape is a symbol of fertility and sometimes also possibility. Lost time and lost possibility but still a lingering hope.

In my photos I insert myself into the landscape, I am the pattern, I am at this place, spreading like a fungus, or water seeping into the surrounding. The ticking sound in the video, time. Life time, turning the pages quickly forward and then backwards again to try and get time back. Wallowing in the past. Turn back the pages. The future when you are young is so slow to come, never fast enough. Always wishing to be older until you are eighteen, and then older still. Then there is losing time. you just live, missing out on all the things you later decide you should have done. Making all the mistakes that at the time are just decisions or in reality no decision. This is the best time, youth, and I didn't do the things I should have done. Or at least I tell myself so now. Enjoying myself more and working more. Maybe. Does it matter. regret. getting old, old, old.

There are so far a few possibilities of titles for my diamond patterns in my art. *Bozo* is the main one, the main theme. It's a black and white diamond pattern. The shapes are connected on all sides so that it becomes a grid. it's like the clown costume, the harlequin.

There is also the pattern *Violence* but I don't use it often. It's only the lines, same as *Bozo* but not black filled in. It usually but not always has a few random lines thickened. I thought of a brick wall you hit at the back with a big hammer or just with your hand or head and a few bricks push out a bit at the front.

Kite is more black than *Bozo*. The *Bozo* pattern gets more filled in by inserting smaller black diamonds into the white space.

Last of the original four patterns is *Skin*. It reminded me of snakeskin. Scaly skin. This one is created by making the empty grid and filling all spaces with a smaller black diamond.

Further titles are *Diamond (d)* and *Diamonds,* these I use mostly in my Chinese ink paintings. Often there is only the one empty diamond shape on the paper. I have been very influenced by Chinese ink painting and I especially love the theory behind it. It's a lot about the state you are in while you paint and you have to be a person with spirit otherwise the art is nothing. The soul of the artist gets reflected in the brushwork on paper. The paper is traditionally very fragile and thin but I also use thick western paper. The brushes are sometimes huge. The four treasures in Chinese painting are the brush, the stone, the ink and paper. It's very ritualised. I love it.

You have to be collected and concentrated. I have practised only from books and saw videos and I am by no means any good at it but I do have an affinity and I love so much about it. I think it's marvellously inspiring. I love a lot about the Chinese and Japanese cultures, find them particularly fascinating. Also there are seven shades of black. My diamonds are one of those shades. Black or grey on white.

Another version of my Chinese ink diamond paintings is *Fence*. This does look like a wire fence. The diamonds are interlocking and fill the space. This is similar to *Violence*. I think *Violence* is faded out. It's my least favourite and I don't like the randomness of the thickening lines.

My newest shape is the unconnected diamond pattern. They are floating in space and are either filled in black or left white. *Shards*.

A version of this is where the background is black and the lozenges are white which makes it look like a metal sheet with holes punched out. Very solid. This pattern I call *Punch* and there is *Punch & Judy*. This is cutting out diamonds to make holes in the paper and the cut out diamonds get stuck on the paper too.

The nature of my line and brush work is usually freehand with a few exceptions. I did just recently buy a stencil and also stamps. I do not use rulers because I am a romantic who finds freehand work far more appealing, oh indeed. I see little value in hard edge macho and serious abstraction with all the precision and tools and such. I have the rough touch and like the handmade or handmaid look with all its mistakes and faults.

◆

Diamonds represent eternity and ever reoccurring tidal waves of consciousness. It's a meditation on all things past, present and future.

In an ideal world I would like to be an evil witch who conjures up all the forgotten and deep down dying and screaming memories of the alter ego of the individual, the lost self. When I make my things, my artworks there is little decision making and no artistic anguish. The only struggle is to keep going. I know I make diamonds in all shapes and sizes. I don't even choose colour. It's usually black on white.

If it's not about the artist's virtuosity it has to be about something else. "We are not interested in appearances and we are not interested in skill." (John Latham). The viewer is sucked into a deep hole of plainness. No excitement at all. Nothing to grab onto and not much of an invitation to even keep looking. But if he looks around and decides: I might as well look at this, because I have time, or some other reason, he will experience peace, memory, a dreamlike state with good or bad or hidden issues poking their heads up. It's handmade. It's made by a person. Why did she do this? What's the point? Do we need this in our world? Might as well be nothing. It has been made by a person, me. I made this. I am the creator and I do have a right to express this particular thing, to engage in this particular practise. I can be and generally am dismissed and ignored and or even ridiculed, there are all engagements and intersections of some kind.

My objects, paintings, creations are precious things from a personal place. I am a person. Just like you are a person.

We all have intrinsic value. We are all capable of enacting meaning. There is no too stupid, there is only the fear of inadequacy. The fear that I don't matter. The question of why am I even here. What am I doing here? There is so much stuff already. Why should I make more? Is there an end to the suffering.

I escape into the little private world of me. I make my own museum of curiosities. I will look at this stuff when I am even older than I am now, old hag me. This will be my output, my legacy, my trace across the space of this passing. The smaller, thinner and easier to store the better. I will be an old lady hopefully, sitting on a diamond upholstered chair in a cute dark room with beautiful lighting and surrounded by beautiful objects either bought in a shop or gifted by a friend or one of my children or my husband and I will take out the book I haven't looked at for forty years. 100 hours of solitude. lichen. an old little observer's book about lichen covered with diamonds. I will read the poetry and remember the video I made to go with it. I will watch that too, make a cup of tea, do some embroidery or draw more diamonds to pass my time.

Maybe I'll still do Instagram and scanning for my forty year old blog. I still have not managed to ever display any of this stuff anywhere because nobody knows I exist. Nobody thinks it's any good. There is no public here.

Especially these days, with everybody being a creator, god how many MFAs can they hand out... but you have to believe in yourself. I have to believe that my stuff is worthwhile, mainly because it exactly is my stuff. It's possible to keep doing this, to keep going without knowing why. Without thinking it's even any good. Real artist or not real art, faker. Everybody is allowed to do it. Have you heard of this thing, a rumour, freedom? What's a real artist anyway. I am a real artist. Am the real artist.

I journey along my artistic process to make my life better. If nobody ever looks it's fine, 'cause what's it got to do with them anyway? I owe it to myself. I have to do it for myself. This is to make my own world. And I choose diamonds. I am filling my world with diamonds.

I see a small rectangular lid on the pavement outside my

house. It's on the way to school. It's down to the left from where I live. Outside one of the big housing estates. Quite ugly surroundings really, the ghettos of the poor. We do have a few trees. Almost no shops or cafes or bakeries or even places to hang out. Just housing estates jammed one against the next and lots of new apartment blocks being build where things have been pulled to the ground and reduced to rubble. Sometimes it really stinks of old rotting concrete or something dangerous for the lungs. I would like to draw or stamp black diamonds on all this. I could make a stencil actually and spray paint it. That would be nice and quick.

I would like to paint the inside of my shed with diamonds. There are so many things in that little shed there is no other place to put it all really. I'll have to find a place to put everything, then paint it and furnish it with relevant items and use it as a location for photography. Mainly to take photos of myself but maybe also for other things. Before I get older, while I am getting old. A record of time.

I am working on a little embroidery on linen. Just the one

shape in black. I would like to make a massive one, two by three meters and hang it on a wall. That would take me one million years to complete.

◆

The possibly messy appearance of my work, that's something. A recurrent idea or thought or nagging whisper. It's an event.

It looks like it should be precise and hard edged geometric art, black and white, diamonds. But it often gets messy. It's all handmade and quite rough at times. The glue on the diamond collages is a normal Pritt glue stick and the ink sometimes gets smudged. I am happy to get things done and I am not bothered too much by messy execution. I am considering staining my embroidery with tea patches and paint over it with acrylic or oil paint. The entire perfection and neatness of Bridget Riley is very far from what I do. I guess nobody even would think there is something there in common but I state it anyway.

What I am doing is different to op art. My diamonds are more like a spreading and crawling over the surface, a spreading of myself. An insertion, a sneaky one, a persistence of not wanting to go under the surface without anybody noticing, a desperate trying to leave traces of myself behind. Of myself at this point in time at this age, the older I get the more evidence I will have of myself, a document of disappearing. It's a memory of my younger self. If it's the same subject, the diamonds, it hangs together as one.

I made so much art in the decade after my graduation from the Slade Art School in London. There were always different styles and different media. I could not find what I wanted to make and what I wanted to be. It was all disjointed and randomly stopped. I still have some work, most of it I burned or tore up and dumped. Especially the big works, no mercy for them. But I cannot refer to it, connect it to my present self.

My diamond work is numbered with dates next to the title, it is part of the title. It's a firm statement about time. On this day of this year I was 39 years old and now I am 64. I think it took me so long to find this because I needed more time. It's hard to think about time when you are in your twenties and even thirties. Time is nothing then. You just live. It's only when time is slipping through your fingers and you realise you are slowly running out and signs of age start to appear on your face that it becomes something much more solid.

The diamonds are myself. Every little one a train of thought, all the things going through my head while I am doing this repetitive and seemingly easy work. Anyone can do it. They might get bored though. All my time buried in this. All my energy dispersed in this. I can measure it with a diamond gauge. It's a payment. Coins.

The look is so plain and unchallenging. Simple structure, like a piece of fabric ready to be made into a garment. Not a thing in itself. Not something, not a painting. But it is, really. It is a painting or a drawing. These items are resting places for your eyes, baths for your restless cogitations. They allow you to think about yourself. Look inside, hear the emptiness. Get upset, angry at the audacity of its patheticism. Roll your eyes and don't bother looking. It's a beautiful decoration for your house. Nice and clean in form and concept, but sometimes maybe with some dirt and mistakes in it. Lots of laziness to love. I have made it. It's me. I am great and wonderful and unique and so amazing. Oh yeah.

It bothers me how there is all this photographic art where the heads are replaced with other things. It's stupid and it's naff. When I do that I keep the face. Keep faces.

I only draw diamonds because it makes me happy to do so. I am sorry if the picture doesn't tell a story. Maybe it can? I do want to move people, want to make them feel something. That's the important thing in life. Feeling emotion. Even the bad ones are alright. There is no good without the bad. Boring boring diamonds but they can look delicate. Special care taken to make a pattern design, simple and basic. Life as simple and basic. A plain decoration. It's nothing like the head by Auerbach with the thick paint. David Bowie's favourite painting apparently.

Oh. I like it if I have an emotional experience when I look at a painting. Which ones do that for me? A Cy Twombly, so emotional, fragile. Van Gogh and Monet, the waterlilies and Matisse overwhelming. The American expressionists are not emotional but bold and strong, invigorating. Robert Motherwell, Barnet Newman, Rothko. Is it the size, is it the macho.

What is good art? I don't know. There is lots of bad art. I know that.

Tick tack tick tack, time passes. I know this too. My children get older before my eyes. I waste my time making "art". Is it art? Who says it is? To many pictures and bad paintings are being made everywhere. Just here in London alone. How many studios how many artists? I make more too, I'm complicit. I have to have my own project. It's personal and mine. It's a diamond mine. It's how I spend my time and what I decided to do with my life.

It's not that this was the obvious path, enacting the choice of art. My obvious and set path by my mother was to run an inn in the Austrian mountains. Up there they don't even know that art exists, that it's a thing. I am not sure my mother has ever stepped foot into an art gallery or museum her entire life. It's simply not something that matters where I come from. In fact it's something that positively doesn't matter. Just like everything else. Hold on a second. It does matter that you have a job and earn money. To have a job that doesn't earn money is not possible. That's a hobby.

If you make something by hand it's different to any other process that involves intervention or prosthetics. If you write a sentence on a piece of paper it's very different from writing it on the computer. There is a bit of the person left on the page if it's handwritten. It's far more personal. The personality shines through. It has soul. That's why I usually make things by hand.

Diamond Frances says:
Art cannot be impersonal. It has to be personal. Especially in this day and age.

◆

Diamonds diamonds diamonds diamonds. Diamonds are everywhere around me and I pick them up with my hands and they fall through my fingers making clack clack sounds. I am sitting in a dark place with thousands of diamonds. It is a deep mine. There is a flash light somewhere which helps me see. The diamonds are raw and cloudy, not shiny as when cut. They are not shiny at all. They are muddy stones. It's interesting how we found out about those and how much we love them. I think they protect us from all evil. All precious stones do and semi precious ones too. But if you only have a tiny little rock on you it won't make a whole lot of difference. You have to have a good amount. A good sized one at the very least, and a selection ideally.

That's why I make diamonds.

But it's just the same name. It's a geometric shape. It's nothing. It's not even an interesting pictorial area. Repetition. Of he same shape, some shape, and I call it diamonds. I name it. What a farce, what a nonsense. It's the same name nonetheless.

The precious and hardest stone and the abstracted shape. They are the same thing. When I think of one I also think of the other. And thinking is if not the same as being then in some essential way superior and very necessary. That's were fantasy comes from, imagination. Fantasy is the most precious thing in the world. Without imagination a person is nothing much. There is no richness and no freedom. We have to treasure imagination. Our society doesn't treasure it, barely values it. With fantasy you can have vision. You can make things, exciting things. Without it we are stuck in uncreative ruts with a horizon as near as our noses.

Poor poor people without diamonds in their lives. We are lucky some of us are producing it still, ahem yes as in me. Pay attention to your self and a vision instead of wondering what to buy next and where to holiday next to make your friends jealous and have a big fake happy face and no meaning to be found anywhere. Like this we end up in a society full of uninspiring deadheads. In a very bad way, not in a good way.

It's all bullshit. The handmade nature of my diamond. It's beautiful and lovely. I love the way my works look sometimes. But some look bad. I have one hanging up on my wall and I don't think it's very good. I have to take it down. The diamonds are connected, quite small, ink on paper, there is a black mount around it, that might be the problem or one of them. The pattern goes to the edge. It really doesn't look right. It should go.

There is another field of diamonds right next to it and it's much better. It is very similar even so. The frame is smaller and the drawing comes right to the edge of the frame without any mounting and the diamonds are bigger and that's it. That's the difference but it looks much nicer. There is no story there in either of those works. No story at all, so it cannot connect to people. It cannot make them feel things and get inside the body to change it. But it does have an effect. I think so. Of course it's art because it's about the process. Process matters. Maybe none of this is true.

David Bowie had an art collection. I think it's now sold. I

bet lots of people wanted it even more because David Bowie liked it and it was hanging in his house. It's called provenance. Those pictures have lived with David Bowie. I would like those paintings too. I can see how people would want to own those. What happened to the money? Who gets the money? His family? They didn't want his art? Maybe he would have liked it better if the pictures stayed together as the David Bowie Art Collection, but it doesn't matter to him because he is dead now. Just like Michael Jackson and Prince and Zaha Hadid. Even if you are famous and rich you will die. We all die. Do we all live?

The paintings of his collection, as featured in a magazine article, were all proper paintings. Figurative mainly but also abstract but they had materiality. It seemed to be about something concrete, not something intangible. He collected paintings with narrative. No hard edge abstraction and he didn't like contemporary art. He had proper paintings by artists like Frank Auerbach and the St. Ives group. Well, there is a story now surrounding that art. Not just the works but the David story. Him owning it.

I hope my diamonds can have a story. I want them to have an effect inside the body. I want them to evoke feeling. I like the way they look. I have tried so many things and I really do like the way it looks and I like to make it. That's something. I want my practise to have value and be important to some extent. I like it and I want more of it and maybe that's enough. I think it is. I hope my art comes from the right place inside of me. I hope it's honest which I am not sure of, I cannot be sure. I don't know what I'll do in the future and for how long I can keep going. You cannot know those things beforehand. I know that, especially I know that. I think it's personal. It makes me happy that's enough for me.

I don't want to be self limiting. I don't want to be narrow minded or stuck in a rut or stubborn and not open to new creative urges I might have, suppressing them because of other ideas of consistency and identity.

I pray I am on the right path because I want to be a real artist.

I must be different from the rest of the world because they keep telling me, reminding me, insisting, that it is not enough. There must be people out there who are similar to me, with kind of similar ideas and values and thoughts? We are all different but there must be groups of types. I want to find my group. Please, group, where are you?

Is there anybody out there? I want some sort of connection. I want you to like my art and I don't want you to say I suck. These days I hear nothing at all. No peep nor squeak. Not even an acknowledgement of having seen it because nobody has ever noticed it. There is so much and I am in a pile. A huge fat pile of artistic production and I am at the bottom in the sludge with the worthless. I am doomed.

Oh no! So boring. Diamonds. Such a plain shape. Who cares. So what, oh dear. Let me tell you. I represent freedom and polarity and a zen like state with the atrocities that happen around the world in mind. It's an escape. Makes me think of peace and better things. I am not showing more stories. Horrible and shocking stories from the news. Blood and axes like in a Stephen King film. I didn't read the books. I only saw the movies. The landscape and setting. The hotel Jack Nicholson is driving too. The twin girls. I cannot remember it all but it left an impression. It must be twenty five years ago since I watched those movies, back in Austria and dubbed into German. There is also the one with the lady in the house. Misery. That brutal solitude and landscape is what I am imagining. A place in America, not Austria with lots of trees, fresh air, quite cold. Beautiful nature. And I have a desk or a studio. I have a studio so I can do big brutal paintings too. I love doing big messy paintings. Now I do smaller delicate things. I don't know if I would still enjoy the big mess but I think I would. I am pretty sure actually. But that's a different story. I stick to the diamonds, not the horror. There is sometimes some. Horror.

I am not painting idyll or excitement or the little joys, the garden the nature the loved person at home, the adventure girl fighting evil, the brave and strong or the down and out person on the street. no stories. only a feeling. an absence of feeling. It's zen-like in the harlequin pattern. The clown clothing pattern in black and white or just the shape if they are not connected. Drawn and painted, cut, stitched. It is a feeling, an escape, a serenity, a rejection of participation. There is something somewhere inside to connect to, a story of interiority.

Those diamonds mean something. Really. They are precious, precious treasure.

I want to be open, not closed. If you do big messy work you need to either have lots of storage or sell them. It's hard to keep making big bulky paintings and then what? Cut it up and throw it out when you move, yes. I did that already, have done it repeatedly. I have destroyed all of my large canvas works. There is nothing left pre-2010. It's all gone in the rubbish. Maybe four or five sketchbooks and some canvases that weren't in my house at the time and are now lost to me. I wonder if they still live?

That's old and out of date. And I'll never get paid. I make things now. Small to go in my little folder. To keep and look at when I am older. I want a lovely big collection of a big effort of diamonds on a lot of paper. Billions of diamonds.

My money, my legacy. Possibly also to go into the rubbish when they clear out my stuff because I am gone and stiff and a corpse now. There is only so much you can keep. This book seems to be about death. I always end up talking about death. This is the book of death.

Almost forty now. In two months I will be forty years old and all I think about is death. I am hungry. I want to eat some breakfast. Bacon and egg muffins with Worcestershire Sauce, a cup of tea, orange juice and a marmalade toast. That's a life. I love that. I want that breakfast. Now. It's Saturday.

◆

I start painting. Please get me some black tar thick ink. I want to get started. I want to make a big one. A big canvas and then maybe I should throw some sparkles on it. Or maybe I cut it. Maybe I can cut it and then glue it onto a new one. Then put some more black ink on it. Or thick rich oil paint. Fat oil. Let it dry with cracks and pebbles and wax encrusted.

It's a huge studio I work in, in my mind. Concrete floor. Big old factory style windows and not very toasty. I have a big gas heater. That's the only way to get some warmth in here. I have an old carpet and a droopy couch. A desk too because sometimes I do precise and little work. But not clean, no nothing is clean. Sometimes splashes end up on things, marks I didn't predict. That's quite fine. I think it's alright. Accidents are accepted.

I love all the black marks.

There are other artists in the building of course. I know them just a bit. From walking into the same building and seeing them in hallways. Not too sure what they do. No wait let's change that, pebble/people contact. Hang on. That's a lie. It's not true. We all know each other well, us artists in the building. Go and sit in each other's studio and chat about our work and projects. It's always so amazing. I get on very well with all of them and on Fridays we go to the pub together. I bring my three kids, naturally. One is autistic plus other things too. She is nine, doesn't talk but sometimes makes very loud shouting noises. AAAAAhhhhh! She does hit people if there is a problem and the little one three years old gets angry so easily, annoyed if things don't go his way. And the oldest one, ten almost eleven, he says weird stuff sometimes and he might not get what he is doing in this place. My husband is alienated amongst all the people and we struggle to ignore the kids. So, we have to leave early, nothing unusual. A great Friday.

When I stand in the rain and it's not too cold it's pretty good. Sometimes I do that to wash off all the diamonds that over time get stuck on me. When it stops raining I go back to the spot and pick them all up, put them in a special container to keep for ten years and then I want to make something new from them. Probably I'll need glue. Construct a diamond collage.

I make diamond collages from fashion magazines. I cut out any pages with diamonds on them. Usually it's clothing but sometimes other things. Architectural backdrops, handbags, jewellery. When I watch movies and TV shows I always look for them, the diamonds. I see them everywhere.

On ties, upholstery, very often as a part of rooms, wall decoration or iron wrought fences. Diamonds are everywhere around us. It's a very popular decorative pattern. Really it gets used everywhere. It's like, a sign of civilisation. Manmade but can obviously be found in nature too. I don't see the natural ones that much but I do watch TV and look at magazines. If I concentrate on nature more I bet I'd be surprised how much there is out there.

I am also working on an embroidery project. At the moment I am making a 40cm square piece. I'm filling it with black diamonds, stitched. I want to dip it in tea at places to dye a section and then paint thinnish paint over the surface. Oil or acrylic black or white. The embroidery takes a very long time. I want it to be still visible. I don't want to totally overpaint it. I looks lovely. I would also like to make a huge one. Two by three metres. Maybe just leave it stitched. No messing it up. I am not sure yet. Maybe it's more beautiful with only the embroidery.

I have produced a number of diamond books. Old second hand books transformed into diamond poetry. I white out most of the text and keep some words and pictures. Decorate the book's photographs or picture plates with diamonds and cover the rest of the text with diamonds. It's a new book. A poetry book illuminated with diamonds. They take a long time to make, more than 100 hours of work. That's why I call them 100 hours of solitude.

Drawing happens in solitude or next to other people but still in solitude. You can draw together on one page but it's still you and your pen and them and theirs. You could use somebody else's hand then maybe it's not so much about solitude. Me left to my own thoughts. Thinking about what's appearing right in front of me. Watching my lines, how they colour and alter the surface. I also think about other things while I draw, my mind meandering. The past, the future, a person, could be anything. I call it 100 hours of solitude. There is a book I know of. Read it. It has a similar title that's why it's relevant. One hundred years of solitude by Gabriel García Márquez. I am reading it again. I read it when I go to bed. I am always very tired when I go to bed and reading makes me even more tired, also if I read in the daytime I might need a nap just a few lines in. I am a very slow reader. Sometimes I have to reread the last paragraph either because I am not sure if I understood everything or because I especially liked it and want to read it again or sometimes for no reason at all.

I am reading Márquez again because I don't remember anything about it. My teacher brought me lots of books to the hospital when I broke my ankles and back. I read it then, in German translation. I didn't read it with my brain, just with my eyes. Couldn't remember much about it so I decided to reread it and I like it. Anyway, I like the unreal magical bits in the book. I like how Rebecca has a compulsion for eating earth. She stuffs it in and then gets sick. I do not have a clear image of what those people look like and I do get confused about who is who because their names are similar. Especially the men of the family have all pretty much the same name. They all start with the letter A. That's confusing.

The next book I am planning to decorate is about the weather. The last one was about lichen. I did not even know about lichen before I started it. I love lichen now. It's plant like growth on trees and stones and benches, walls. It's not moss. Lichen comes in different colours and grows very very slowly. It's fascinating. I love lichen now. It's a brilliant occupation to look for lichen when out and about and I can recommend it to anyone. You should try it yourself.

I have so many projects. I want to cover pavement lids. Not all of them are suitable but some even have a diamond pattern on it. I would like to paint only black diamonds on it. No white, that would be too eye-catching. It should be very subtle. I'd love to start around where I live, do one on my school run. I would look at it every day and maybe other people notice it too. That would be nice. I'd have to use some type of permanent paint for it to last as long as possible.

I'd like to make a metal structure, a big slightly bent rectangle in a dark metal ideally rusty metal with my *Bozo* pattern, touching diamonds. One is the metal and the other is a hole. Or maybe it would be *Punch*. Diamonds punched out of metal or stone. a big diamond sculpture huge in the landscape. public art. by Diamond Frances.

Another brilliant idea is a billboard. A hand painted billboard. *Bozo* again in black and white. I would be so happy and proud if people could see my diamonds in the world. Most likely they wouldn't notice it at all, ideally, it would confuse them. I like to confuse people. It's basically a decorative and inoffensive pattern without any obvious message. I am not sure it could offend anybody apart from them thinking it's a waste of space for something more important. Taking the place of something with a message. My message is that. My diamond decoration takes the place of all the possible messages, inhabits it, destroys it. I think it's valuable. It doesn't have to be preaching or taking itself too important. I don't like it if people take themselves too seriously. I live here too. I am a person. Those are my diamond patterns.

That's pretty much all of my projects at the moment. Drawing and painting. Collage, embroidery, cutting paper and a fantasy of public art in my mind.

Sometimes I wonder where all the diamonds go. In the

muck digging for them is the only thing that helps me. I find three or four and I am so dirty and stinky after. I smell for an entire week even with scrubbing and rubbing. It's good though. I stink and sit on my table. I draw more and my paper stinks too. Everybody is disgusted and leaves the room. They cannot stand it. I go. I go outside for a walk. If you are outside the smell doesn't fill the room. Like a rotten body it is much better outside. It still stinks the same but there is always fresh air around. Water lilies come from the stinking swamp and the most beautiful flower emerges. That's what happens when I make diamond art. It's destiny and important for humanity, or not. My little contribution.

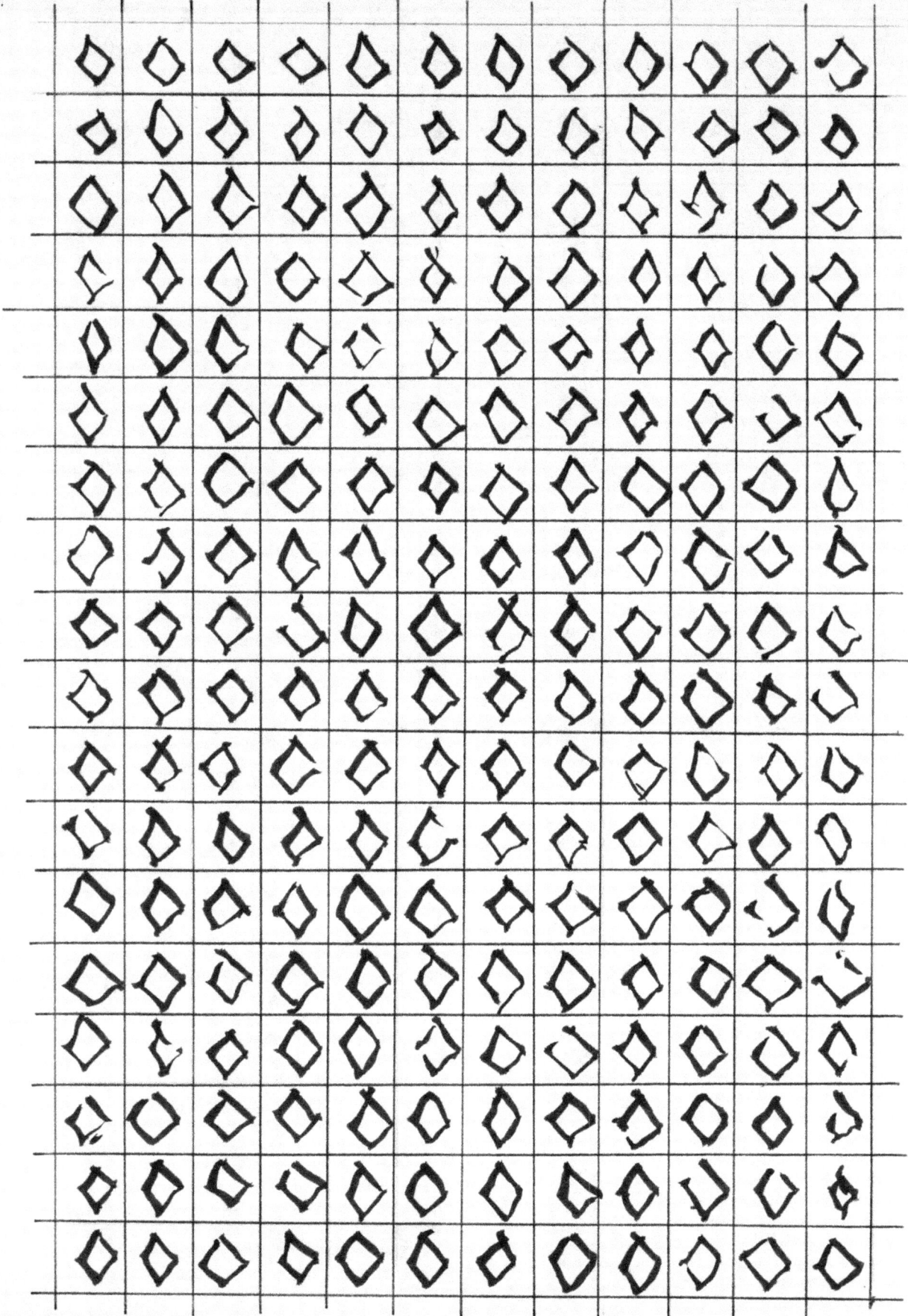

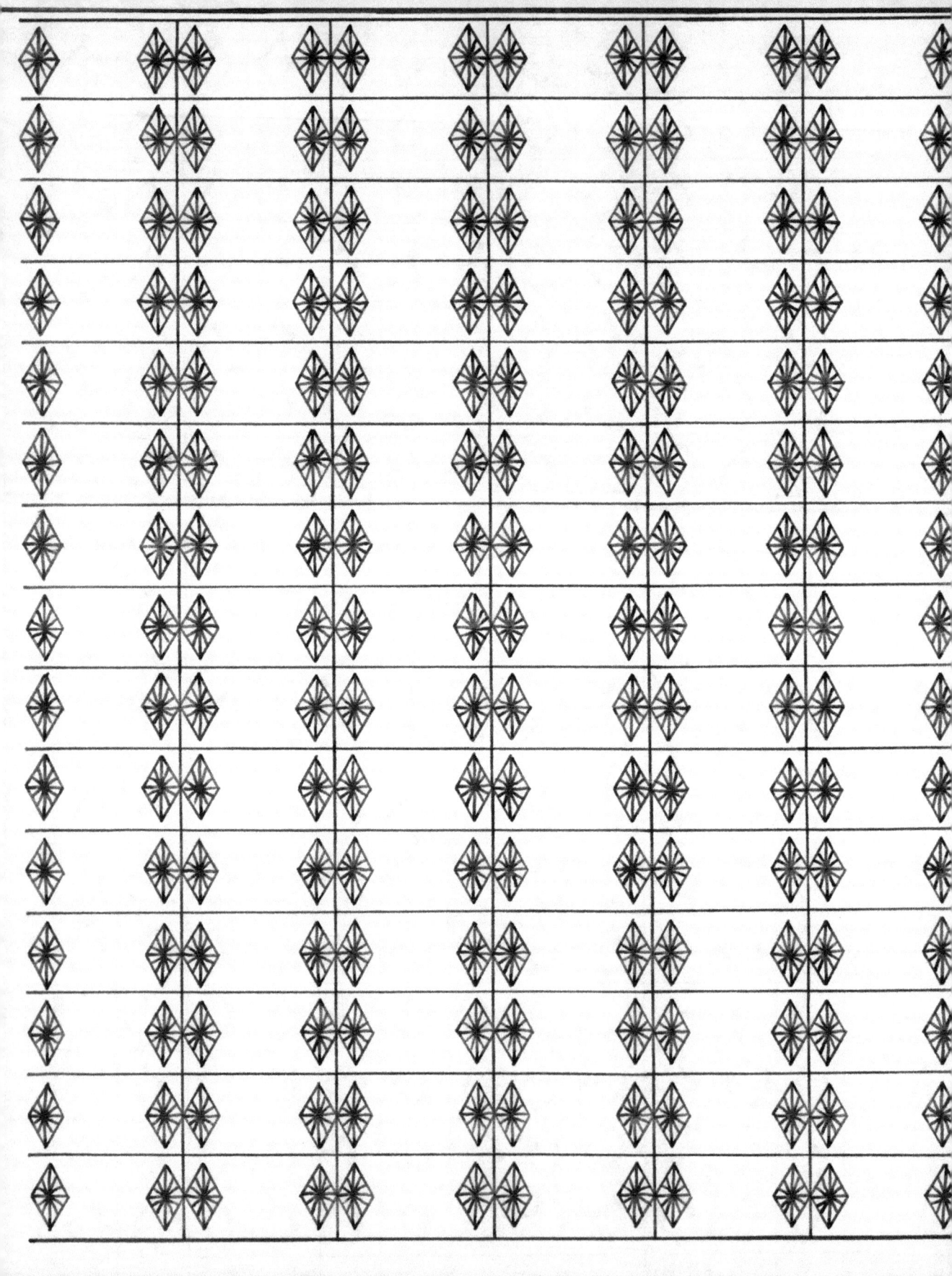

OREBODY

In the forest, the eternal forest of evanescence, diamonds are everywhere. The sparkling kind, real ones from the earth. The strongest thing that can cut everything, slice open all materials. The sparkling and tinkling of the elaborate headdress I am wearing. A queen, small and fragile, distant. Everybody bows in awe. They have only the basic things to live. It's all quite dark. There is only very little light. When the sun does show a bit it's the most beautiful sight.

The men hunt. Getting food is a major occupation. The women bake bread, sometimes sugary bread with dried fruit. There is sweet honey but not much as it must be found in the forests. Meat gets cooked at a central place where everybody comes together. If a big animal gets killed the entire village has a feast, fire roaring in half darkness.

Some occupations within the village don't directly produce

anything and are useless in a sense. These people, dancers and musicians, have to be looked after by the rest of the villagers, be provided with food and shelter. They are happy to do so because all inhabitants perceive a direct benefit of these types of people. They are there for entertainment and unexplainable, indistinct existential reasons. The dancers are more like medicine men, they go into a frenzy and take hallucinogenics. They can be male or female.

There are weavers, dressmakers, bakers, butchers, carpenters, farmers. Only real professions, no fake ones. All boys and girls have to learn and help with embroidery for the dressmakers and weavers. It's an honourable occupation but many are relieved of their obligations as soon as it becomes clear that they have no talent or interest. There are many different patterns with specific meanings. Depending on role, age and standing in the village, everyone wears specific colours and patterns. They mark and code themselves. They have many old traditions and one generation teaches it to the next.

The queen gets special garments with beautiful embroidery

and delicate and precious fabrics. She wears them to show to her people their own brilliance. She comes to visit four times a year for the special seasonal celebrations, dance, music and food. Everybody loves it when she comes to watch because normally she is not seen. The queen lives isolated in the forest in a very basic house. She has three helpers who come to visit at certain times, otherwise she is all by herself.

She has magical qualities and powers but she cannot use them to get food. She is looked after by the village. She would not survive long without their help. Her days are spent wandering the forest enacting her charms. Sometimes she journeys farther. She does not have any codified obligations. Her role is simply to make things. She draws on paper and does her own embroidery. It's considered magical when the queen makes things and they get stored in a special place. The repository is a secret house in the middle of the forest. It's made from concrete and has skilful geometric patterned wooden carvings on the door. There's a big lock on the outside but it doesn't need a key. A very few people can open the repository door lock.

Inside the queen's repository are little windows so one can see by natural light. Massive wooden carved drawers with mother of pearl inlay line the walls. All the diamond drawings are stored inside. There's still more space for more.

Across one huge wall is a huge framed canvas where each year the queen inscribes a diamond, these are the markings of time. It's goes back 1000 years. Each queen does the same. They draw in black ink. Diamonds. There are also objects, sculptures, all have diamond shapes.

Each queen has a special headdress, very high. They have diamond ornaments hanging on very thin chains. They are stored in the repository too in glass fronted cabinets. Each one makes a different noise, a peculiar tone. Nobody knows where the headdresses come from or who makes them, the queens don't. Every queen finds hers out in nature, in the wild forest, and keeps it to wear for ceremonial appearances. It's the most magical item a queen owns.

It brings good luck and happiness when a queen appears in her headdress. The villagers love their queen and they put a lot of effort into making beautiful things and special nutritious food for her. There is also a village elder, a man or woman, simply whomever is the oldest. Usually it is a woman. They are very wise and they make all the decisions for the future of the village, the daily affairs.

Sometimes they have to go to war because there are other clans. Sometimes there is war when the food gets scarce. Weather fluctuates and there is not enough food for everybody, then things get tough. There are wild beasts in the forest who come closer to the villages and put them in danger. Sometimes the beasts kill children who go out too far to play or are careless. Not only children. Hunters and gatherers too. Life in the village can be dangerous. There is a lot of beauty in the struggles and tragedies of life.

In absolute solitude and under great pressure the queen receives her magic from a special diamond place. It makes the earth vibrate and there is a beautiful singing in the air, very faint and distant. The sky lights up just a tiny bit more.

It is only temporary. Time moves in a perpendicular not linear way. It's not like our world. This world is called Blythe.

◆

The diamond tribe lives in the rocks and mountains of Shiki. They live in eternal darkness and only the light of the diamond gives them light.

The theories and stories of interstellar interconnection are of great importance here. At the time of the apocalypse there was a huge clash of titans and the biggest of galactic wars wiped out most of the inhabitants. There were few survivors who suffered memory loss. They had to rebuild a new world without knowledge of previous life. This was a great opportunity to start over again but the same things happened. It seems to be hardwired. Fear is too.

Certain humans rise to a select position that makes them power hungry and greedy. Their minds and spirit corrupt so severely that they are only capable of caring and scheming for themselves and close members of their families. They rarely think about the greater good or higher values. They turn into evil brain eating monsters. Loose all humanity. There are lots of them. And they don't look any different to the normal humans. It's a disaster for humanity.

Titanic cleansing rises.

The diamond documents and diamond artefacts produced over time are the unknown treasures and protectors of the diamond tribe. They are a hidden heat source that keeps the world energised. The world has greater energy and a protection shield because of the work of individuals who remain in isolation in order to produce these treasures. Their papers and objects need to be protected otherwise the human races shrink, mutate into just monsters and loose their souls. The diamond documents enable compassion, love, happiness and generosity in its people.

◆

Hidden diamond world, or any world, it doesn't seem to

matter which, I had enough of it all. No more stories. The stories are all the same, the same in every world, even the parallel ones. Good guy bad guy and happy ending or disaster or open ended. Power and play and danger and fight. Happy lives and anguish. It keeps going and going, recycling and resetting. Stories make us feel and make us cry and be happy and laugh but still. I don't want it. I want my peace. I want it all gone. Nothing. Something different, something else. I want a different world.

The diamond princess is the talisman of the new. She is the element of moment. Everything she does concerns itself neither with past nor future nor even the present. She always lives in pure moment. She never makes plans and does not seek the bigger picture. She is the bringer of happiness. Seeing the bigger picture or worrying about the future, especially the quest for future security is the killer of moment and killer of life. She is a breath of fresh air. She removes all extraneous baggage and worry. She brings luck and health to all people. Not everybody can have her. That's not possible. Only one diamond at any time for any people. That's the rule.

The burden of the past and the burden of the future and the absent now. It's all a mess and it weighs the inhabitants down like a bag of bricks on the back. Like a million bricks all over their bodies. The answer lies in the diamond moment.

She sits and does her work. She draws more diamonds. It all happens in the moment. You can look at the artefacts and old papers from the past. It's beautiful. It is beyond meaning.

◆

At the brink of dawn there is a white beautiful unicorn standing at the edge of the forest looking right at me. It's quite dark but the air is fresh and there is glitter in the air with the wind and the noise of the wind in the trees. The unicorn makes a noise through her nostrils and is so full of pulsating energy. I can see all the muscles in her body flexing and rippling.

She runs off into the forest and I follow. I see diamonds floating in the air shining bright, all around. I hold my hand out to touch. They are little stones but they float and they are bright with light. At touch their light dims and can be plucked from their place. I collect some in my bag.

I walk through the beautiful twilight forest, dew on leaves sparkles. No human has ever been here before me. I hear the unicorn running and sometimes catch a glimpse through the trees and foliage. I walk fast. I come to a cleft cave opening. I duck within. It is big inside and cut from crystals. That's were the unicorn went, deep into the dark beyond.

As I walk water tinkles on the ground and a dim light permeating the walls light my way. I keep walking. The air is fresh on my face. I hear drops of water falling. Quiet fills the gaps between drips. I touch the cold stone walls.

A bend in the tight path leads into a cavernous opening and more and more light floods the space. Sparkles fill the air. It's like exiting the cave but also never leaving it, a whole world within the enclosed space.

It's bright with light and a perfect temperature, a strange diamond light. There are lots of trees and plants with silver leaves and I see my unicorn nuzzling more of its kind. They must live here, I think. They eat some diamond grass.

I look around, walking slowly through the strange plants. Sitting down on the mossy soft ground I close my eyes. I wake back in my normal bed, in the normal world. I should go there more often is the first thought I have. I look in my bag on the floor in the corner. It's filled with diamond rocks from the dream world. I go to my workshop and want to drill little holes in them to hang them up with string. No drill can get through. I need diamond tips.

I found a cave here in my world that is not of this world. I suspend my otherworld objects from the ceiling. When the wind blows through them they clank and tinkle together making a noise, a diamond song.

Magic stones from my friend the unicorn hang from my

ceiling and play chimes to me. She with her pure white coat and flowing mane is my only friend. I am a lonely individual, alienated from this world called everyday.

The only way to communicate with my friend and her siblings in the unicorn world is to sit and draw diamonds. For ever and ever I sit cramped and hunched at my desk to put diamonds in the treasure chest for my people yet to come. It is my secret occupation and allows them others to live in the moment. The diamond moment.

This process is old. Queens have produced these artefacts for centuries and they are a protection charm for galactic civilisation. Without this work people would kill each other from greed for money and power and simple selfishness. Without these diamond texts stored in a secret place in the forests of eternity there would be no access at all for humans to the sacred spaces of sincerity, peace, compassion and love.

Whomever sees a diamond paper or object receives a bit of magic dust sprinkled upon them. It gives them peace and unity for the moment and from the moment. It lays an invisible layer upon consciousness. The closer a people live to a storehouse of diamond texts the more blessed they are. There are a few spread throughout the planet. Some are very old indeed and even though they are not updated or worked on they still have an effect. They bring the possibility of happiness.

Transcribing the diamond communiques from the unicorn world is very important work. The queens are often forced to realign themselves to fit into their new role. This can involve painful and difficult actions concerning their lives. Often, this means leaving the old life behind, cutting ties with the family. Transformation with an old life attached is impossible. The queen needs to gain absolute freedom but it also means a totally solitary life. Most people don't want that and they often struggle. They want happiness from their home and friends instead. There is a great price to pay to become a queen and it's not something one can or should choose. Nobody would. It's predestined, it is not a choice at all. It is necessity.

After the first violent steps there is even more struggle for a princess on the crystal path. The initial acceptance was only one step and the apprentice has to cross many more hurdles. General society dislikes and condemns all activity and efforts of the unicorn princesses. She often faces indifference and outright rejection. Until she has firmly established her true calling and transformed herself into a different being, content and accepting of her role as princess she will have to endure a lot of suffering but interspersed with moments of true happiness.

If there was no queen, everybody would be just fine. But the queen is dependent and needs the people to supply food and shelter, make clothes and look after her basic needs otherwise she will die. There are many people who are not happy with this and want it to stop. They think real resources are being wasted on the queen with her useless production and instead should be spent on making the rich people richer because they want even more money than they already have. Strangely even the poor want that too. The rich who see no value in the diamonds of the crystal unicorn princesses want to save the planet all for themselves. Only the rich matter. Everybody thinks it's a good idea. Especially the other rich and influential friends of course, but somehow the poor workers too.

Many of the unicorns may die. The money symbionts are under the strong hypnotic influence of the abstract named money. They are in fact possessed by a spirit they cannot understand, and they are mere tools of bigger forces than them, trapped in a dimensionally thin superficial life with surface pleasures. These half-lived are the shop-bought ones with plastic zombie lives. They have many friends and everybody thinks they are great. Every construct of the economic machine brings with them their own preordained life satisfaction. They are very pleased and taken with themselves. The pain, struggle and happiness of the diamond princesses is something they can never ever know.

◆

In the distance there is a lone cowboy. He rides towards the horizon with his hat on his head upon his horse. He trots slowly. There is nothing around him apart from desert sand and he travels a forgotten highway. In the distance there is a high mountain range.

I stop my car quite far back, well behind the cowboy. I sit and observe. I get out and start walking down the ribbon of black tar towards him. I take my purse, my phone and a bottle of water with me. And a peanut snack bar.

He moves faster than me and after some time walking I have lost him to the distance. I am all by myself and the car is still in sight but really far back. I keep walking. The mountain range looms closer and closer. I keep walking and eventually I arrive at the foot of the mountain. Before me is a huge block of stone, massive. I find a shady place to sit and take out my snack bar, eat it.

Only about a third of my water remains so I take a few little sips. I look out across the desert and flat straight road, nothing. My car is only a wavering dot. I wonder where the cowboy has gone. I wonder If he was ever there in the first place.

I take out my phone and listen to a song or two with my eyes closed against the glare. The White Stripes, Truth doesn't make a Noise and Leonard Cohen, Lover, Lover, Lover. I switch off the music. If I was still smoking I would have a cigarette right now.

The light dims as the sun sinks and I start walking again. My feet hurt and I start slowly but the pain diminishes the more I walk. I have to make it back to my car before it gets dark. Luckily I can still see it, a shape on the horizon. There is not much water left but I have another bottle in the car. I'll be alright.

◆

Diamond is my best friend. I am her best friend too. I am so happy because I wanted a best friend all my life but it never quite worked out for me. I was usually the one who was more into the friendship and then I got hurt and disappointed because I realised they didn't like me as much as I would have liked them to. Now I have Diamond.

101

Diamond is like me and we are perfect together. It's almost as if we were the same person. She is always there for me. I talk to her. She makes half of my art. It's so nice to be able to work side by side. She wears all the crazy outfits. Trying to get diamond design outfits and accessories. Her hair is short and grey. It's a beautiful shade of soft blue grey. It's her natural colour. Everybody else with this sort of colour had it dyed but not her.

She is from a different world. Diamond is a bit taller than me. Just a tiny bit. She walks with me when I need to leave the house. Sometimes I take Jesus with me too, especially if I need extra protection or courage but often I forget and I go all by myself.

Diamond and I eat ice cream together, a big pot full of it. We watch daytime TV together. I love to watch good advertisements, those are the best. But there are always so many bad ones. Diamond doesn't enjoy the ads much, instead she likes talk shows. Sometimes we sit outside in the garden and work on our big embroidery project, she at one end, I at the other. It's a very time consuming and long term project. She is sure that one day it will hang somewhere for display. In an embassy maybe or a museum. And somebody will pay for it, pay big so that we can have money just like those other people who get money for whatever they are doing, making ads and TV shows. Diamond is absolutely certain. I tell her it doesn't matter that much and that I am not so sure about it as she is. She gets outraged and insists that all people should get paid for their work so they don't have to take the role of scum of society.

Sometimes Diamond gets sad and angry about the situation. She gets up and puts some soil in her mouth, chewing it. Sitting on the ground, her face dirty, she keeps chewing and chewing and then swallows it. She gets up and goes over to the water hose, washes her face splashing water in her eyes and goes inside. I keep stitching. Eventually she comes back out and sits down again, picks up the embroidery. I tell her she shouldn't do that, it's not good for her health. She says she knows but she cannot help it and that's how she gets rid of her anger. It kind of helps me getting rid of my anger too. She really is my best friend. I love Diamond.

◆

The diamond queen is in her forest dwelling. She just woke up. It's 4.30am and she brews herself a tea. There is little noise in the forest and dawn is yet to break. She drinks her tea in a chair on her front veranda and absorbs all the dark shades of green and black into her body.

Her dwelling is a raised glass box. All around the bottom storey is beautifully carved ancient wood.

She prepares to leave. Her working area is elsewhere. She puts on her simple working clothes, a black, long sleeved roll neck shirt and a big black coarse woollen skirt that hangs all the way to the floor with dark grey diamond patterned knee length socks and a chunky knit medium grey cardigan with a V opening and big horn buttons. Her shoes are bulky and sturdy because of the forest floor and she wears an off-white heavy cape with faint diamond stitching to protect herself form the wind and rain. The cape and skirt have pockets, deep pockets.

The queen likes and needs big pockets in all her clothes, mainly for her hands but also for other little items she finds along the way. She wears a big cap with diamond crochet made from cotton in summer and wool in winter otherwise her ears get cold. The cape has a big hood too. Before leaving her house each day she takes a juicy and weird cake, her preparatory medicine, and eats it before she leaves.

The workhouse is close to the mountains, about a forty minute walk. Her workshop is built into the side of a massive rock. It looks modern by local standards. She unlocks the big metal door with a blink of her left eye.

Inside, in the main room is a large wooden desk. There are special storage rooms with big chest of drawers and complicated locks. Down a corridor towards the back away from the natural light are storerooms filled with art materials, anything she could want or dream of. Further back is also a printing studio filled with many machines of mechanical and digital design. Robotic assistants wait dormant until she engages processes that require helpers.

She takes off her coat and shoes, changes into her indoor work slippers, sits down on her sofa and stares out through the massive glass walls of the main room. Then she rises and moves to her desk and starts drawing.

At midday there is a knock on the door. A girl from the village brings lunch. The queen is happy to see her and they sit down together in the soft grass outside. The queen doesn't talk, just eats her lunch in silence. The girl watches her. When the queen is finished the girl puts the bowl back in her bag and takes out a bottle with two cups. The queen pours a drink for the girl and herself. They drink and sit and now talk a little. When they are finished with their drinks the girl puts everything back in the bag, smiles and says goodbye. The queen smiles too, thanks her and waves, watching her walk off.

She stays seated and feels the bliss of a full belly.

Eventually the queen lies down on the grass and takes her daily nap. Wonderful days. When she wakes up she goes inside to continue her work until the end of the day. If her drawing is not finished she puts it away in a drawer and continues the next day.

The queen puts on her coat and walks back to her house. Dinner is in a bag in the downstairs area, in the wooden carved room. She takes it upstairs, gets ready and changes into her floppy lounge wear. She sits down on her couch to eat her dinner and puts the empty bowl in the bag. She is almost always alone but she talks to the birds who come and visit her. She goes to bed and sleeps until the morning. She wishes she could have a pet, a diamond dragon. A few queens in the past were given diamond dragons.

Today is the day of celebration in the village. This happens four times a year to celebrate the seasons. The queen does not work today. It takes her all day to get ready. She will have to go for her ceremonial walk in the forest to the house with all her artefacts and special clothing, jewellery, shoes and headwear, all kept in a secure place next to the workhouse. Some of these things are ancient.

The queen has her own special headwear and cannot wear anybody else's. It has been made especially for her with her specific sound. The tingling clinking diamonds are made out of a very fine material nobody knows what it is. Not glass and not metal but something like it. She washes her hair, creams her entire body with a special strong smelling herbal balm, puts on make-up, thick black eye make up. It's a precise procedure and she knows exactly what to do. She has done it so many times. Nobody has ever shown her what to do. The first time she came here and saw all the pots and containers, brushes and pencils it made sense to her and she just used everything available. No confusion or uncertainty, more like she was born with the ritual already inside. Imprinted. She loves doing this. Her clothing is literally out of this world. It's a welcome and necessary change to her daily routines without anybody around her. She is devoted to a total life of solitude but these events are important for her, without them it's possible she would go mad.

Her special headdress makes a beautiful sound, mesmerising to all who hear it. It even puts the queen herself in a vacuous, clean state. She is transported by the continuous sound of a different world as she quickly walks with small, fast steps the path to the garage with her vehicle inside. Her car is carved but not from wood, the whole thing including the bronze clad wheels is made from whitish bone. Where such massive bones came from, what creature could have such bone none knew. The queen waits by the door in silence, a sound, rustling in the forest, and noises, two men talking casually while they walk. They have come to be the motive force for her chariot.

They bow as deep as they can considering they are wearing an impressive costume with massive horns on their heads. She makes the sign on the foreheads slipping them through the cracks of the world and tells them to rise. The men wear carved wooden masks scary devil masks with huge animal horns. They look terrifying with their costumes of long animal hair. One is wearing a dirty white goat hair costume, the other dark brown. The queen sees those costumes every year but it's always quite an event. Shivers of excitement down the spine and looking forward to a big social gathering. It's the mid winter celebration and the men are made up like this to scare away all evil spirits. They also reek of old animal fat. It's an assault on all senses.

The queen contrasts strongly with these fear inducing creatures. She seems angel like but dressed in black not white, pure black with sparkles of diamonds and intricate diamond patterns embroidered all over her clothing.

It takes them about one hour to get to the village and big bells and chains attached to these petrifying creatures make a lot of noise. These two men have to be the strongest of the village. It takes a huge amount of effort to pull the queen along in her chariot, for that long. Everything has been prepared. There is music, drums and harps, people everywhere and all the villagers wear their special celebration clothing, beaded caps and hats and capes and decorated jackets in different colours with intricate patterns. When the queen's chariot arrives everybody watches. She is formally greeted by the village eldest. It's somebody new, different from the last celebration when she was greeted by a woman. She must have died. She was ancient. The man is dressed with many layers of preciously embroidered heavy garments and an elaborate headwear made from metal, long tangling beads, wool and coloured stones. He smiles at her and bows low. He accompanies her to the ceremonial throne. From her vantage on the raised dais the queen sits and watches the celebrations unfold and gets course after course of food and wine and other liquors brought to her on lavish trays. The village elder and his wife sit with her but they talk very little. It's not uncomfortable silence it's just the traditional procedure. The queens never talk much. They are usually socially awkward because of their constant isolation. She does not feel comfortable with social politeness and has no practise in it. She nods and smiles about comments from the elder and his wife but very much retains her otherworldly appearance and distant air.

Her visitations have a profound effect on the villagers. They will end the feast with magical aura imbued on them, energetic and spiritual. It gives them cultural feeling, refined community and a sense that there is more to existence than satisfying the basic needs of a human being. The ceremony of the diamond queen is essential for sanity, internal prosperity and long term peace and contentment. The villagers may be more or less aware of these effects but they are confident in the feeling that lasts inside themselves for months.

When the festival ends the queen is escorted back to her house. The eldest thanks her for her visit and all the people clap and cheer when she leaves. It takes just as long to get back. The two masked men drop the queen off at her home and bring the chariot back to the other place. She is alone again. She takes all her festive attire off and has a hot bath. These public appearances drain her and make her happy at the same time. It's good for her to have different types of days. Not always the same routines. It takes her a while to order her thoughts and all the excitement. She sits for an hour in her living area looking out into the darkness before she is ready to finally drift off to sleep.

The day after the event is another day off. The queen's body is still intoxicated from all the special herbal infused food and drinks she ingested. Her head is still buzzing full of impressions from the previous day, also there is an uneasy nagging feeling about the village elder. He seemed distant and slightly irritated behind his facade. This is an unsuitable state for her to work in. She has to wait another day. The next day everything is back to normal and the queen happily continues her daily work.

Weeks have gone by since the celebration and the day starts as every day but at lunchtime, there is no child and there is no food. There is no dinner at her home and the next day there is no food either. The queen makes do with tea and little snacks she has in her house. She wonders what is going on, she has panic attacks and is shivering all over her body. The possible implications are catastrophic for her. Sometimes she manages to calm herself down and tries to find plausible explanations. She is talking to flowers and animals around her, ants and bugs on the forest ground. The fact that she is really hungry doesn't help her state of mind. All week there is no food and no emissary from the village. She has no choice but to try and walk to the village but she doesn't even really know the way. She was always escorted, never went there before. She has to speak with the eldest. She could feel a slight tension at the celebration but she had no idea this was going to happen. There is still a chance it's just a mistake or other problem of some sort. She needs to find out. Hopefully she won't get lost on the way.

The villagers only see the queen at festivals unless they are in service. Children playing at the outskirts recognise her first and are excited to see her. She doesn't pay anybody much attention. She looks frail and weak in her ordinary clothes, the majesty and mystery of the celebration being absent. The queen looks like one of them, nothing special. The new village elder steps out of his tent to greet her and invites her in. He lets her know explicitly what she suspects in her heart. He is collected and distant, matter-of-factly. She sits in front of him and looks right at him while he talks. After he is finished she gets up and leaves the tent. She didn't say a word to him. The forever oracle tells every queen to expect this.

The new view on things is that the queen's work deep in the forest is useless and pointless. They have decided to let go of this unnecessary fluff, these stupid works for the unknown archive. The village elder has decided it is time to let go of her. Times are hard and they simply cannot afford to keep this going, the resources are needed elsewhere.

Internally distraught she leaves the place. Old women are sobbing and waving at her and children are running next to her trying to touch her. A small gathering escorts her out of the village, there are shouts and cries and beatings.

The queen becomes very skinny over time. She is not equipped to feed herself and lives mainly on berries, greens, tubers and mushrooms she finds in the forest. She gets weaker and weaker by the day. Sleeps more and more. She is too weak and hungry now to continue her work.

One day an old woman arrives. She brings food. The old woman is very sad and has tears in her eyes the entire time the queen devours the food set before her like an animal. There is the usual bottle with two glasses. The queen does what she always did, she pours the drink and they sit together drinking. The old woman remembers this from when she was a child, serving the queen of diamonds. This time the queen only manages a smile. The old woman packs up and leaves with a heaviness in her heart. She promises to come again tomorrow.

The queen takes a nap. She is happy because she has had some food. The next day, the old woman comes again. It's less food than the day before and the old woman looks weak. The long walk is too long for an old woman and the food was meant for her. She tries to smile at the queen but she is also still very sad and embarrassed and upset about the situation. What a terrible thing to have to live through, to picture the queen like this, abandoned and cast out, skinny and weak, an old lady trying to sustain an exhausted and frail queen. Once more the queen takes out the drink. This time there are two bottles. They drink the first bottle and sit together in silence.

When it's finished, the old lady packs up and takes out the second bottle and leaves a glass. She gets up and goes,

116

touches the queen on her arm, smiles with tears in her eyes and sobs goodbye, walks off slowly. The queen looks at her until she is out of sight. She opens the bottle and drinks until it's all gone. She lays down for her nap, leaves falling silently around her. The queen knows that the old lady will not be coming back. She has consumed her last meal. She fades into a deep sleep and knows she won't be getting up. The last day of a long succession of diamond queens. There is a soft rustling noise. A diamond dragon appears from the forest. He walks up to the sleeping queen and lays down next to her.

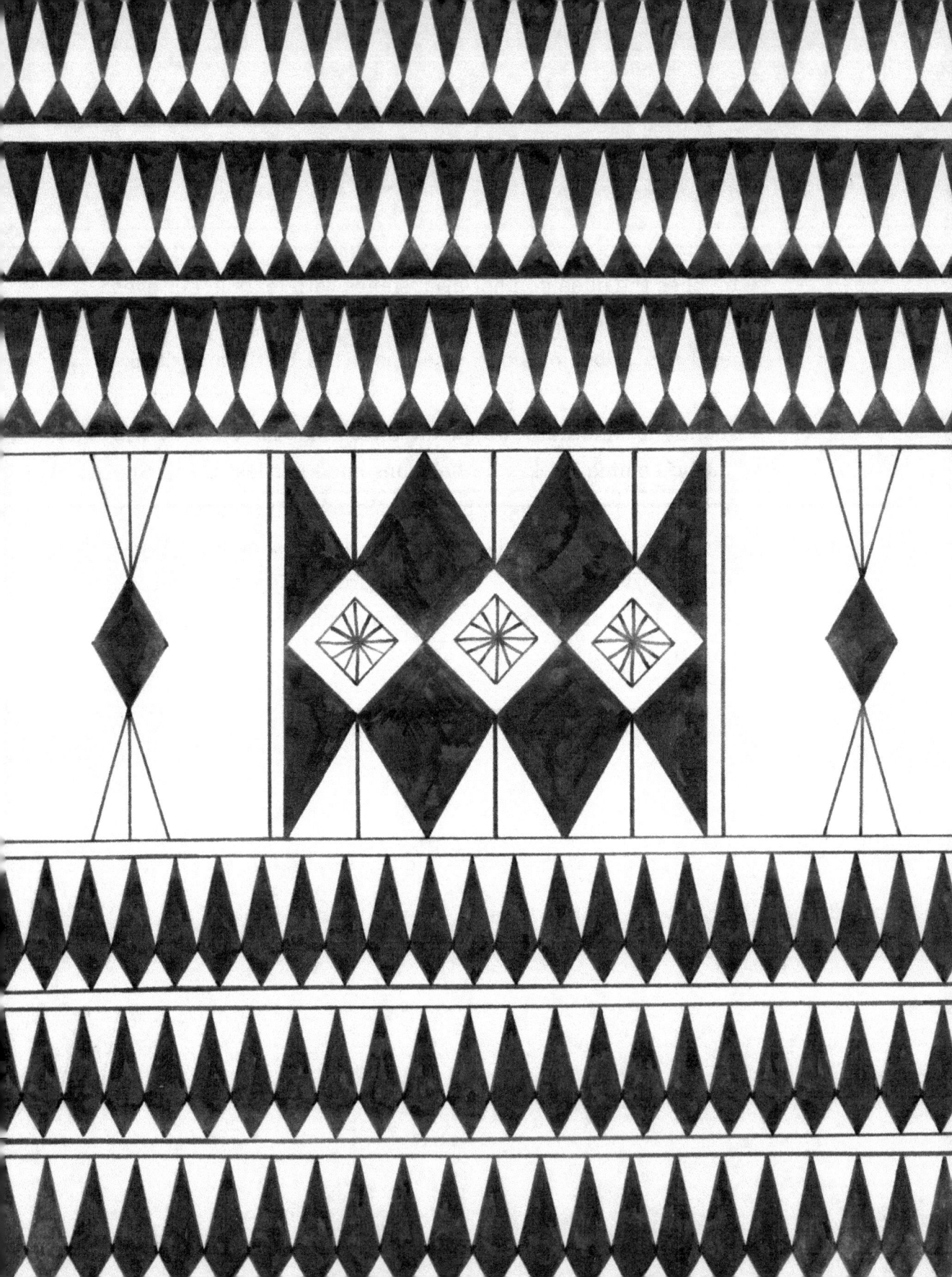

EXTRACTION

Diamonds are the basis of my work. I would like to cover as many surfaces as possible with this simple design, simple and plain. Like a Chinese farmer in a remote village in the distances far from civilisation. The landscape and the mist of the past and future. A simple life within the simple compounds of the person.

◆

Can you like and dislike the same thing at once? I think so. Immediate gratification and a constant running against the clock, confusion about what to do and where to look. Where do you look? Making things that nobody can see, will see. A book full of diamonds, can you sit there and be interested, keep turning the page, if everything is the same? There is variation but it's small, differentiation by fractions. We have better things to look at, all the beautiful and captivating images. Tick tack tick tack, the diamonds are coming.

◆

This is my life. It's the weirdest thing and I know my parents and sisters hate it, deeply. They shake their heads and say I should get a proper job. What a waste of time and what has any of it to do with this life anyway? Nothing, obviously.

◆

The lucky ones have passion, born with it or attained later. It doesn't matter which. Some people are lucky. They have the passion. I always admired that, being passionate about things. Everything was always the same to me. Nothing matters. Nothing ever mattered to anybody. I am like them, I was born there, I come from there. That place. They put it inside me. It's their fault. Not mine. Just sit there and do the things that have to be done. No inspiration, no passion. It's a life in motion. We share a life, the simple togetherness. Making something precious was something we never did, ever. I am in for the fight. It's the only thing that matters.

◆

Things happened and I made decisions. I put them in frames. It put me on a path of realisation, realising how important world building is. It's the only thing I have, I know that now. I cannot live in these other worlds build by everyone else. It's not right, not for me. I have to make my own world to live in and decide what it's like. I want my world plain and simple. I don't want to fill the world with more meaningless imagery. I will have diamonds around me. There will still be a million other things because we all have so many things. Food and objects and furniture and tumble dryers. It's a slow process and once I do fill my life with more diamonds all around, maybe I'll go mad slightly. The more personal and intricate a world, the more complete and complex it is, the more the person whose world it is can live in it and almost totally retreat from the common shared world.

◆

What would happen if everyone was actively building and living in their own world? How would community look?

◆

The younger a person is the less likely it is that she/he is already building her/his own world. Some never even start. The younger a person is the less intricate, complete, personal and specific her/his world is, and the more cluttered with foreign influences it is. At a certain stage in a person's life there needs to be a thorough clean out. Some ancient or fanatic world builders are totally into their constructions and totally whacked out of sync with the common. Another name for this is utopia. Some of these old ones do have to come out into shared spaces. Especially if other people want to connect to and experience their worlds. That's what is commonly called success.

◆

Young passionate people can have more intricate worlds than much older lazy people.

♦

The question is not where do I want to live. The question is where do they let me live being the person I am.

♦

Art is made to document existence. It is a desire to share experience and feeling. It might not be essential to everyone's life but it is essential to some sort of collective sanity and it can never be totally eradicated. Art and fantasy bridge gaps from our everyday life to something else. It's a special sort of communication, also the broadest medium of communication available to humans. It enables a reaching out and enables connections.

♦

If life is a sequence of runs, running around like a mad pig trying to grab frantically everything around us we can, luxury items, ideas and ideals, or worse even, grab from the shared and generic world called cliché, then life will necessarily be sick and poor. I see a lot of that, everybody wanting the same life, wanting some version of a life they saw on TV or in a magazine, on Instagram. The ready made great life from the catalogue. Being famous, having that kind of house, looking a certain way, going to important events with other important people, getting invited to rich people's houses and parties, buying expensive clothes. We need lots of money and want everybody to kiss our ass because we are just so amazing. This vision is the prepackaged image, the proper reflection of a sick and poor life. I promote its rejection and destruction. That's why, make art.

◆

There is a problem in western schools, really there is a problem everywhere. We do maths and reading and writing, fair enough but lots of meaningless generalities or specific trivialities that do not do anything for the further evolvement and general wholesomeness of the individual. We don't have a basic education about what makes life good, the essence of health and prosperity. Moral education needs to be addressed, like Confucius. Chinese children do learn about these things. Maybe not about the individual as world builder and prime creator but at least about codes of proper conduct and morals and how to live well in harmony with others. That's why the Chinese are the new world power, the old world power too really. We should all learn from them or move over there. And they eat weird food sometimes but it's great. I can't say anything about specifics, for example all the problems Ai Weiwei has.

◆

Friendships need looking after, tending, like plants. They are never perfect but when I was little I thought they were. I always waited for my perfect friend to arrive, especially when I started a new school. She never came and I stopped looking. I got it wrong. I am idealistic and that has consequences. I think that's ok.

◆

Our father always told us we were talking rubbish when we opened our mouths to say something. That didn't help me. I thought I was not capable of thoughts worth expressing. I evolved into not a big talker. No talking at all sometimes, too shy and worried I might say something stupid. The older I get the more I realise it doesn't matter if you say something stupid. I still think I am stupid and I think I have no opinion on anything. I am talking for women here and now because I am one. I am scared of revealing my stupidity. If my new goal can be to be the stupidest person in the room I am free of all fears and free to say things. I wished I could do that more. Maybe I can, maybe I am?

◆

I am an artist and I have something to say. I usually say it without words. I am writing this here and it's quite fascinating to give my voice expression. I do speak. I am doing it. I want to tell my father, to tell all fathers, we can do it.

◆

If you do create and you die and all your stuff gets dumped and smashed, that's fine. You still did your job. Others might think it's crap even with your death to crown it. That's to be expected for some of us. Expected. I think of the strength and courage it takes to pull myself up from the mud and wipe away the boot prints on the back of my clothes and keep going. It's tough. I make diamonds. They are the hardest thing in the world.

◆

There are too many artists. The problem is that 'artist' is listed in the catalogue 'desirable ready made life styles'.

◆

Beware, floating to the top does not mean you and your work are are any good. It just means you floated to the top. Now you are lucky enough to make money but that doesn't mean you are good, it means you made some money. This has to do with the ant effect. One walks this way and everybody else follows. It also has a lot to do with the advertising industry. The ant effect and the advertising industry, these are not good art. Production meetings, finances and accounting arrangements, licensing agreements, employing and managing a team, inventory, stock, tour schedules, more businesswoman than artist. More business than art. How can any of this be any good for life, good for the world?

◆

Lucky me, I am free. I can do whatever I like. Nobody is on my case. I can take a day off when I want. I can change my focus and do collage one day and embroidery the next. I am a total island unto to myself. Forget John Donne! I have freedom but for a price... Ah, you getting this, the economic price, because it's all economics right? Obscurity, cash deficit, bankruptcy, food banks, second hand clothes, balloons for birthdays... Forget economics! I am one of the too many artists and whatever happens it will be bad, because all the economists said so. Lucky me, I am free.

◆

Diamonds partly symbolise the tragic and final end to an episode of my life that's over. From the depths of my subconsciousness I am digging up the half dead and disgusting creatures, vampiric entities, that have been sucking the life-juice out of me. We are born with all the energy and all the purity. Then you are either lucky and fit your surroundings well and get nurtured and develop quickly and prosper or there is an irreconcilable clash with your setting and there will be a lot of struggle. Hard struggle. Unhappiness and sickness and addiction. Some of us never make it out. Dispelling the demons of a fractured beginning is a long and painful path.

◆

In the aftermath of total and absolute depression the only remedy is a big diamond nap and a big cup of hot chocolate with diamond sprinkles and some daytime TV on a cosy couch with my favourite black and white cashmere diamond blanket ensconcing me. Ideally the couch would be diamond upholstered too. Overcoming a sad face just needs time. Sometimes we need to go to bed for three days and not come out. Ask Bukowski.

◆

The original artist is an individual who is maladjusted to society. She does not feel at ease in a general and encompassing way and struggles to interact with other individuals. She is very sensitive and highly perceptive. She is a loner due to her chronic maladjustment. Often she works obsessively because of an overwhelming urge that comes from deep within. Being an original artist has not one thing to do with good networking skills, possessing a friendly disposition and easygoing nature nor widespread social acceptance and interpersonal camaraderie. The original artist does not have a predisposition for business.

◆

I eat diamond apples on the diamond grass. I seek for real stone diamonds under the diamond carpet. I open the diamond can with a diamond cutter. I eat diamond beans on diamond toast. I love the diamond couch with the houseplant there and my diamond garden with all the diamond council housing projects I am surrounded by. The diamond sun shines only for me and the diamond tinkling noise is comforting above my head. I am happy to see all the beautiful diamonds.

◆

Apart from the total absence of things, there is always the possibility of going to live in the eternal abyss or on Mars. Diamond space travel is a pure construct of imagination. It's what we don't use anymore or never did or only very few people do and it makes us a very much poorer society because of it. Where has all the original thought gone?

◆

Out of total enragement at life and subsequent engagement with the deepest depth of the psyche there comes a convulsion and a scream of disbelief and desperate struggle. Absolute and total bliss and a future full of love and flowers and sunshine arises to fill the void. Struggle remains as a simple part of life.

◆

Smooth running the entire way is a lopsided and unhealthy perspective and also unsatisfactory as it implies not only an imperfection of view but an incapacity to see beyond.

◆

Out of distress and hard work and rejection and bile running out of all your bodily openings there will be a diamond production and you will excrete diamonds and this will not hurt anybody. Not even yourself. Out of the darkness and into the light you will build your own dwelling from dried dung and also for your family. The children will run around innocent in nature and play like you used to when you were little wearing simple and plain clothes. All the birds and the other animals surround you and the warm bliss of the sun shines right into your soul. The eternal sunshine of the soul and the true meaning and reason for why humans live on this planet in the here and now has been fulfilled. We build with rotten pewter stench procrastinate procreate.

◆

A lot of humans on here. And every single one is destroying it. One day planet earth will explode with all of us still on it. Maybe we should be stones. We are heading for disaster. If I look at a bigger picture, things get out of hand and start to look extremely bad. I need to look somewhere else. Things can look really good. But not here if it's like this. I'd love to be optimistic. I am, especially about the future. But is this what the people really need? Discard shallow consumerism. Look for real things and you'll wipe out the rich deciders. They can get what you have. And they'd be better off too. Meanies.

◆

We are all important. Nobody is worth more or less than

any other person. We all have the same rights. Nobody is above or below anybody else, no matter where they come from, what gender they are, how smart they are and how much money they have. Everybody knows this but nobody lives by these rules.

◆

Midlife crisis occurs when you realise you are running out of time and the things you thought would happen haven't happened and they are not on the horizon either. Crisis arises from the fact that you are a person you didn't want to be, living a life you didn't want. Usually this means you are living a life that is different from what you imagined in your youth. Often, the life we imagine in our youth is vague and general, some story of amazing success. That happens to an awful lot of people. Pretty much everybody. I have to let go of all these fantasies, these lunatic fantasies of mine which are not even real and concentrate on what I have. I realise that my life right now is as good as it gets. These unhappy days are actually my happiest ones. There is no happier future for me, this is all I have and actually, I am getting older every day.

◆

It's like I am out on a ship in the middle of an eternal ocean. It's not the earth because there would be land sometimes, here is no land.

◆

But remember, art is not business. Don't let it bite you in the backside. Focus on the self is of utmost importance. Don't look elsewhere and don't look where the money is. That's a fake fantasy of happiness. Everybody knows that, right?

◆

Who ever said life was easy? Um... no one? There are wolves and hyenas out there and they want to eat you. Watch out. You have to fight and they have to eat. You are a princess and pure diamond. Nobody will bring you down

because you are as strong as you need to be. Is believing
that easy?

◆

I am an idiot.
I am stupid.
I am clever.
I am intelligent.
I am a superstar.
I am arrogant.
I am mean.
I don't like you.
I don't like anybody.
I hate everybody.
I think I am great.
I think everybody hates me.
I think I am stupid.
Where have all my diamonds gone?

◆

What every individual does and thinks makes up a social

psyche. If everybody doesn't care and has no values, no morals, this will be our society. The more of us who are precious about our thoughts and actions, the better this world can be. Everybody's psyche is a part of a whole. It's an energy. It's a fallacy to think that one cannot make a difference. We are all part of the whole and what we do matters. I realise my responsibility. Everybody's psyche is equally strong and has the same effect as everybody else's. We all need to act like this life actually matters. This will make the individual and society happy and provide meaning. This is missing and has been for quite some time now.

♦

The area between some kind of ideal life of a person, their galactic fantasy about themselves, unfortunately always non-existent and the actual reality of that life, that's an interesting area.

This is the area where things go all wrong and what ends up being our actual life. The ideal self is difficult to conceive of, it seems to be continuously out of reach and impossible to get a good grasp on and it's also very vague.

There is a fragile small bridge that a brave person can walk on from one side to the other to close the gap sometimes just for a moment to see your faint galactic fantasy of yourself a bit clearer.

◆

Crystal Violet. A synthetic violet dye, related to rosaniline, used as a stain in microscopy and as an antiseptic in the treatment of skin infections.

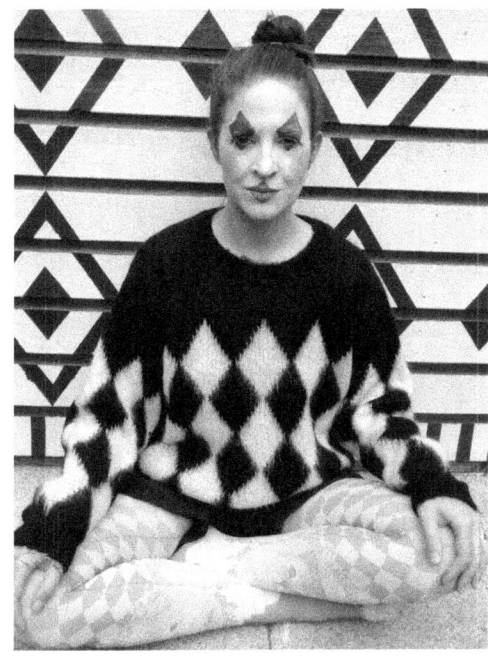

◆ **Diamond Frances** ◆ lives and works in East London with her husband and three children. She was born in the Tyrol, Austria, and graduated from the Slade School of Fine Art in 2005. After a decade of intense experimentation and travelling widely her work in recent years has become more refined and focused. MINE is her first book and it provides detailed background and context to her current art projects and theoretical structures. At the heart of Diamond Frances's work is the concept and realisation of art as a tool for living in a more meaningful way, impelling individuals and society away from commercial money machines and superficial, elitist outlets of consumerist idiocy. Diamond Frances is a pioneer of the old way of doing things.

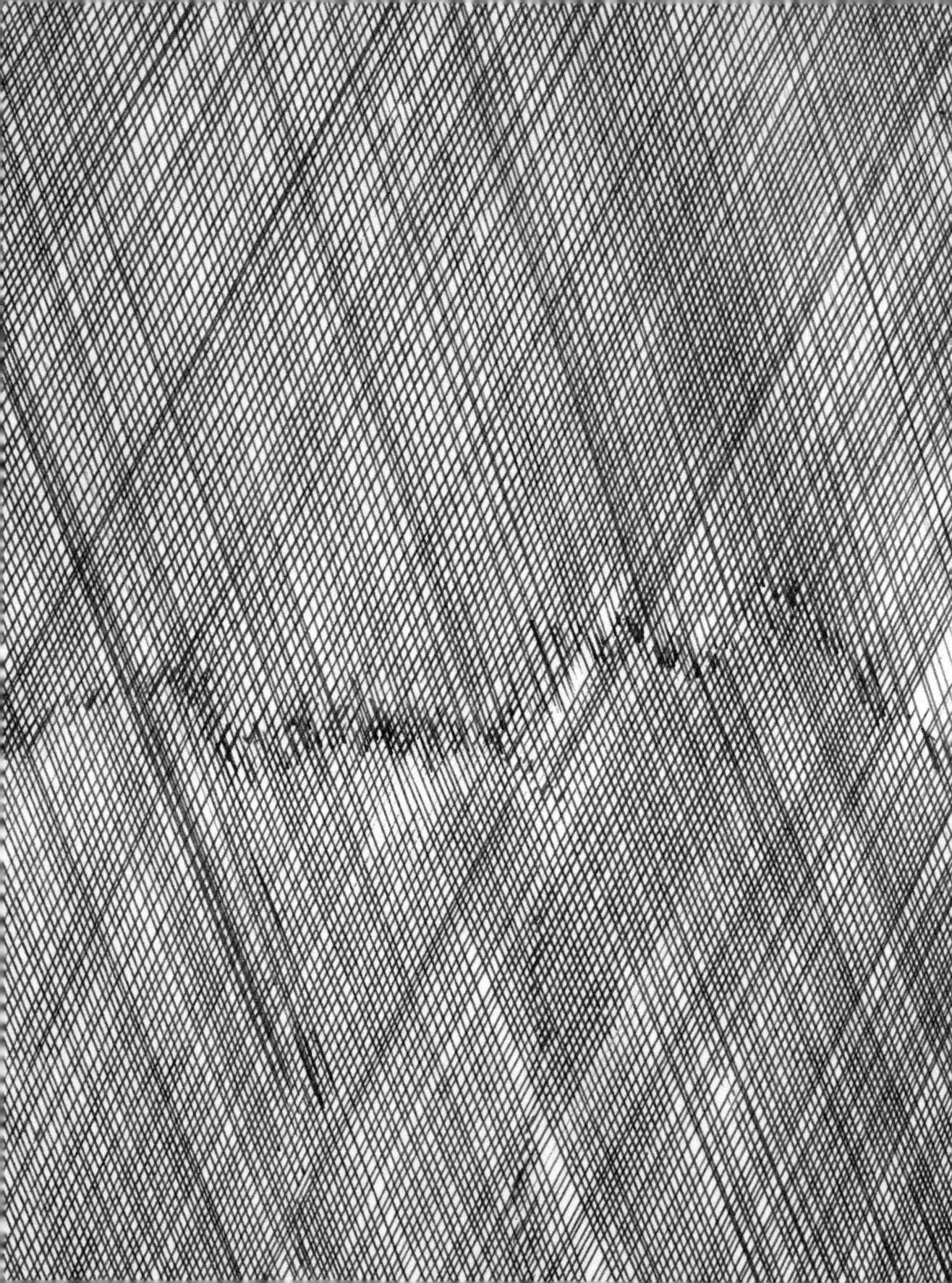

www.ingramcontent.com/pod-product-compliance
Lightning Source LLC
Chambersburg PA
CBHW080248180526
45167CB00006B/2461